Ten Days
in the
Light
of
'Akká

Ten Days in the Light of 'Akká

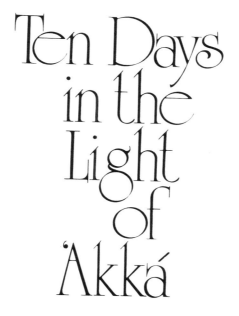

JULIA M. GRUNDY

BAHÁ'Í PUBLISHING TRUST
Wilmette, Illinois 60091

12/97

Library of Congress Cataloging in Publication Data

Grundy, Julia Margaret Kunkle, 1874-
    Ten days in the light of 'Akká.

    First published in 1907 under title: Ten days
in the light of Acca.
    Includes bibliographical references.
    1. Bahaism.   I.   Title.
BP365.G7   1979   297'.89   79-12177
ISBN 0-87743-131-0

Design by John Solarz

Printed in the United States of America

10   9   8   7   6   5   4   3   2   1

C. 1

CONTENTS

v

FOREWORD

Before there were Bahá'í books, pamphlets, period-
icals—before there were, properly speaking, Bahá'í
administrative institutions; before 'Abdu'l-Bahá made
His historic voyage to America; before Shoghi Effendi transmitted to the English speakers of the world
his own sensitive and authoritative translations of the
Writings central to the Bahá'í Faith—there were
Bahá'ís in America. On what spiritual food did they
subsist? As soon as the announcement had been made
at the World Parliament of Religions in 1893, concerning the spiritual sanctity of Bahá'u'lláh, Americans began to explore the new Revelation. Some Persian Bahá'ís came from the Holy Land about that time
to give lessons in the Bahá'í Faith in New York and
Chicago. The first pilgrimage to 'Akká and Haifa, in
1898, was followed by a steady and ever-increasing
stream of Americans intent on hearing the Faith ex-
pounded by 'Abdu'l-Bahá, Whom Bahá'u'lláh had
designated Center of the Covenant. The pilgrims, on
their return to the United States and Canada, conveyed their ardor, enkindled at the feet of the Master,
to their questing compatriots. They did it by word of
mouth, by private letter, by widely circulated and
continually copied and recopied letters, descriptions,
journals, and accounts that went from hand to hand.
Sometimes they published their little books and
pamphlets; and, when the Bahá'í Publishing Society
(predecessor of the present Bahá'í Publishing Trust)

was established in 1902, these travelers' accounts constituted an important part of its output.

But infinitely more important than such publications were the Tablets, or letters, that 'Abdu'l-Bahá sent to the North American pilgrims. He maintained a continuous correspondence with the early believers, who welcomed the Tablets and eagerly, reverently shared them with their friends—by the same means, informal and formal, by which their personal experiences as pilgrims had been shared. The Tablets were written in Persian and were translated into English either in the Holy Land or in America by Persian believers and teachers.

One of the translators of these Tablets was the Master's grandson, Shoghi Effendi, destined by 'Abdu'l-Bahá's Will and Testament to become the Guardian of the Cause of God. There came to be, even before Shoghi Effendi's accession to the Guardianship, a strong sense of the difference between official, authoritative expressions of the thoughts of Bahá'u'lláh and 'Abdu'l-Bahá, on the one hand, and the informal reminiscences of travelers, on the other—of travelers eager to capture the precious words uttered by the Master as He taught the pilgrims—for He always taught; at tea, at lunch, on walks, on expeditions of mercy to the poor, He taught by deeds as well as words. Every minute of the pilgrims' day was a lesson, sometimes concealed to all but the truly sensitive, sometimes apparent to the least gifted. Clearly, in the "pilgrims' notes" (as they came to be called) there was necessarily involved the fallibility of each pilgrim's memory and interpretive capacity. There was a danger that a sentence in a letter, dictated in response to a very particular question, might be generalized far beyond the case to which it was addressed or that an oral lesson, adapted and filtered by the needs of the hearer, become the basis of a doctrine that, emanating from 'Abdu'l-Bahá, would be seen as binding on all believers. Precisely this had happened in Islám: the Traditions, or Ḥadiths—that is, the sayings of Muḥammad as reported by His disciples—had come to represent, for the majority of Muslims, an authority second only to that of the Qur'án itself.

Bahá'u'lláh Himself had made it clear that, as Shoghi Effendi put it in a letter written on his behalf, "only those things that have been revealed in the form of Tablets have a binding power over the friends. Hearsays may be matters of interest but can in no way claim authority" (Bahá'í News, no. 125 [May 1939], 6). Shoghi Effendi was particularly vigilant in such matters and repeatedly warned the friends against accepting hearsay as binding on anyone except him who had heard the Master with his own ears. However that may be, what can be more thrilling, short of the immediate experience, than hearing or reading the account in a pilgrim's own words of his reception in the loving arms of the Master? Who can tire of the description of those penetrating eyes, that warm and merry laughter, the wise brow, the wisps of hair escaping from the confining turban? Surely pilgrims' notes are not binding on us; they cannot be adduced as proof of anything; they cannot provide the basis of a serious, critical analysis of Bahá'í teachings—though the temptation to use them so is sometimes nearly irresistible!—but the sense of 'Abdu'l-Bahá's presence, His quintessential courtesy, His tenderness,

His occasional severity, His powers of intellect and concentration—all these are infinitely precious to Bahá'ís, every one of whom is in love with the Master.

In spite of considerable effort of research, we know practically nothing about the life of Julia M. Grundy. There are records of John M. Grundy, her husband; O. Z. Whitehead, in his chapter on Mr. and Mrs. Howard MacNutt in *Some Early Bahá'ís of the West*, p. 36, mentions Mrs. Grundy as having been in their party of pilgrims in 1905—this is certainly the pilgrimage of which the present book (published in 1907) is a record. She was listed as a Bahá'í in Brooklyn, New York, as late as 1944. After that, no further trace. Some reader of this reëdition is bound to know more, and we shall be grateful for any more information that may be sent to us.

This account of Julia Grundy's pilgrimage to 'Akká tells us more about her than we would probably learn from external sources. *Ten Days in the Light of 'Akká* gives us a glimpse into the life of the Holy Household and introduces us not only into the presence of the Center of the Covenant but also into that of some other persons of lesser degree—but more of that later.

The central object of this account—which appears to be daily notes only slightly organized and barely rewritten for publication—is to enable the pilgrim to share with fellow believers the lessons she heard from the lips of the Master Himself. At this point we must sound once again the customary caveat: "Pilgrims' notes" convey, not the words of 'Abdu'l-Bahá, but the pilgrim's memory and understanding of those words. We must, however, be permitted to inquire as to the degree of reliability of these notes. Two indications appear that seem to confer on them a rather high degree of accuracy.

The first has to do with the lack of evident discrimination in presenting the lessons, whether of 'Abdu'l-Bahá or some of the Persians (or Mr. MacNutt, for that matter) who happened to be at 'Akká. Mrs. Grundy makes very few observations of her own, contenting herself for the most part with a few statements of fact: "'Abdu'l-Bahá sent for me. I found Him in a little room opening from the courtyard. He was sitting upon a raised chair, His beautiful face, majestic in repose and strength, turned toward the only window. He greeted me joyfully. Both the daughters were present. He said. . . ." Yes, her admiration is expressed, but with sobriety and modesty. The sentences are short and direct, and except for the chapters "Visit to the Tomb" and "Visit to the Riḍván" the text consists preponderantly of direct quotations. Although the attributes of 'Abdu'l-Bahá—His beauty, kindness, and so on, are clearly marked, there is no comment or judgment made concerning His words or any other speaker's: the quotations stand on their own, without any attempt on the part of their self-effacing reporter to influence the reader.

It would probably be evident to one quite unacquainted with the principles of the Bahá'í Faith, solely on the basis of the lessons given by the several teachers, that there is a sensible difference between 'Abdu'l-Bahá and all the rest, as to spirituality, intelligence, reason, and sense of structure and rhetoric; and among the rest, there is a clear gradation, my perception of which I have no intention of imposing upon the reader. The fact that those differences leap to the eye is a testimony to the objectivity of the reporter.

Another evidence of accuracy in reporting emerges from the substantively exact correspondence of Mrs. Grundy's version of the lessons of 'Abdu'l-Bahá with the authorized Writings of the Master that have been published since her pilgrimage. Again, comparison with the other teachers serves to confirm the author's faithfulness to the text of the lessons spoken in her presence.

However, there are several points of variance between Julia Grundy's pilgrim's notes and what we know, from authorized Writings, to be either the historical truth of certain events or the doctrine revealed by the principal Figures of the Bahá'í Faith.

For example, the "Mother of the Household" tells (p. 85) the story of a dream that Bahá'u'lláh is supposed to have had when He was six years old. His father, according to this version, consulted a dream interpreter who explained visions "for the Kings." If we refer to *The Dawn-Breakers*, p. 119, however, we learn that it was Bahá'u'lláh's father who had the dream—and there is no indication that the interpreter was attached to the royal court. A small but substantive discrepancy that shows the wisdom of Shoghi Effendi's warning against uncritical confidence in pilgrims' notes.

As to more theoretical—even theological— interpretation, here again there are discrepancies between the discourses of the lesser teachers and those of the Master. Mírzá Asadulláh comes very close to implying that 'Abdu'l-Bahá enjoys direct Revelation: "... His Knowledge has descended from the Invisible Source of Knowledge, and the Holy Spirit is speaking through Him" (p. 98). Yet 'Abdu'l-Bahá, far from ever making such a claim, is quoted in this book as denying most emphatically that He is the returned Christ, in spite of the strong wish of many of His disciples to believe so (see pp. 36–37 in the chapter on "The Manifestation"). Another indication of 'Abdu'l-Bahá's appreciation both of His secondary status compared to that of a Manifestation of God and of the importance of that station as commanding the obedience of all who believe in the Covenant is clearly delineated in the chapter entitled "The Second Coming." On page 62 He establishes a multiple analogy: Moses : Joshua :: Christ : Peter :: Bahá'u'lláh : 'Abdu'l-Bahá, adding that this last authorization of successorship was, unlike the previous one, written in the Manifestation's "own Hand." One should remark that this is not the progressive revelation of the chain of Manifestations; the very different proportion John the Baptist : Christ :: the Báb : Bahá'u'lláh is not in question here. That is the difference between the successorship of Mírzá Yaḥyá to the Báb, and the supersession of the Báb by Bahá'u'lláh. Just as Joshua continues the Mosaic era, and Peter the Christian era, Subḥ-i-Azal was supposed to continue the Bábí Dispensation; and, just as Christ superseded Moses, and Muḥammad, Christ, so Bahá'u'lláh has superseded the Báb. 'Abdu'l-Bahá, by comparing Himself to Joshua and to Peter, and in denying His correspondence to Christ, clearly rules out for Himself the station of Manifestation of God.

It is hard to read the lesson of Badí'u'lláh in the light of hindsight and to retain one's objectivity and thus judge Mrs. Grundy's. Our hindsight comes from having read Shoghi Effendi's *God Passes By*, where Mírzá Badí'u'lláh and his brother Mírzá Díyáu'lláh are identified as Covenant-breakers of the party of the infamous Muḥammad-'Alí. The two brothers vacillated, returned to the Bahá'í fold several times, and ultimately chose to rebel against the Covenant. Obviously, Badí'u'lláh was undergoing one of his episodes of repentance, for he mentions Muḥammad-'Alí with evident disapproval (p. 82). It is impossible to read these words today without at least suspecting Badí'u'lláh of hypocrisy.

The mention of Muḥammad-'Alí recalls to the reader that this pilgrimage took place in a time of great trouble for the Bahá'ís. The sadness that the nefarious activities of the Covenant-breakers occasioned the Master breaks through from time to time in this account (pp. 50, 51), but for the most part He clearly makes of cheerfulness in adversity a law of conduct. With what courage (and foresight!) He proclaims: "If all the world combined against Me, I would still possess this power, and all the world could not take it away from Me. I can fight with this weapon forever and will always be victorious. It is a sword which can never be dulled, a magazine that is always filled." This from the gentle, modest Servant of Bahá shows His other side—His firmness in the calm knowledge of His invincible station and of the power that will always sustain Him.

What do we learn about Julia Grundy? Here is the picture that emerges, for me at least, for I could be proven quite wrong by one who really knew her: She is modest, even fearful, but has the courage of faith. I have the distinct impression that 'Abdu'l-Bahá tried to inspire her with confidence. He succeeded, at least to the extent that she could produce this book. She is earnest, perhaps lacking in humor; it is odd that she never mentions 'Abdu'l-Bahá's love of laughter, a characteristic other pilgrims rarely fail to observe.

That this preface threatens to become longer than the book indicates the power of these pilgrim's notes to stimulate curiosity, imagination, and thought, in spite of their modest mien. They constitute a personal, though not intimate, record and, at the same time, a document of considerable historical value. In them we hear the voice of 'Abdu'l-Bahá through the mind and heart of a good and simple person and once again appreciate His ability tő teach anyone right to the limit of his spiritual and intellectual capacity to learn.

HOWARD GAREY

Ten Days
in the
Light
of
'Akká

INTRODUCTION

I realize that the doors of a new Life are opening within me and that I have been awakened as if from a sleep. Now it seems that never again can I go back to the life which is so trivial, unsatisfying, and without eternal purpose.

It is a supreme pleasure to live in an atmosphere which is all Light. Here I see about me those who have already laid hold upon Immortality, and viewing them I realize that I too am a child of the Kingdom.

I met 'Abdu'l-Bahá shortly after our arrival in the Household. He said, "Blessed are you that the Word of God has reached you and found your soul awake. Blessed it is that the East and the West have met in the Kingdom of God as Christ prophesied." I said, "It is a heavenly privilege to know the Truth and become a child of the Kingdom." He replied, "I hope to meet you in the Spiritual Kingdom." I said, "That will be my wish and desire." He answered, "I will pray for you."

From the Words of 'Abdu'l-Bahá

"Moral life consists in the government of one's self. Immortality is government of a human soul by the Divine Will."

———

"The soul is the Sanctuary of God; Reason is His Throne."

———

"Our Actions reveal what we are, no matter what the tongue speaks."

———

"Every drop of blood shed in the Cause of God will raise up one hundred believers."

"Martyrdom is the supreme test of belief. Great martyrs will arise in this Cause in the years to come. A believer is sometimes called upon to suffer a living martyrdom."

———

"Are miracles performed in this Day?" "Miracles are constantly being performed in the material world about us, yet they make but little impression. Every Prophet has His own particular Mission and function. He does not come merely to perform miracles. People do not trouble themselves about the proof of miracles. The function of a physician is not to make a tree talk."

———

"Be firm in the West! Let the foundation principles of this Truth become deep-rooted. Hold fast until the fullness of Reality comes to you. Christ's Teachings were established largely through the firmness of Paul. Many calamities will befall the believers, but by loving the Cause of God, it will be uplifted in human souls and the believers strengthened. Love one another. Live in Unity under the Tent of God. Firmness and Love make Unity. God will assist all who serve in this Cause."

"Spirit is universal. Man is created in a potential degree of Spirit. Growth is from the mental station into the Spiritual, something like the development from soldier to Commander. God Himself cannot compel the soul to become spiritual. The exercise of a free human will is necessary. We can point the way and furnish the example. We should do little things as well as great things for the Love of God. We should love people because they are God's creatures."

"Are the Manifestations sinless?" "Yes, there must be a standard of perfection for human example."

"Are Manifestations limited?" "They are limited only by the capacity of souls to whom They reveal the Word."

"What becomes of an undeveloped infant's soul?" "It rests with the Mercy of God and through the Eternal Bounty it will not be deprived of that Mercy."

"Will the Tablets and Utterances of Bahá'u'lláh be added to our Bible?" "No, they are a distinct Revelation of God and will form a Book larger than our Bible."

"What will be the future of this Revelation?"
"Know this—that the Revelation of Bahá'u'lláh is the Word of God. There will not be a home which does not contain a believer. Look not at the present. Turn your vision upon the future. All the books written concerning the History of this Revelation number about fifty volumes."

"Will the money of the rich ever be divided among the people without revolution or bloodshed?"
"Will some men amass great fortunes in the future while others remain poor?"
"Will the law prevent this condition of affairs?"
"It will not be possible in the future for men to amass great fortunes by the labor of others. The rich will willingly divide. They will come to this gradually, naturally, by their own volition. It will never be accomplished by war and bloodshed. The ruling power or government cannot treat the rich unjustly. To force them to divide their wealth would be unjust. In the future, proportionately about three-quarters of the profits will go to the workmen and one-quarter to the owner. This condition will prevail in about one century. It will certainly come to pass."

"The Blessed Perfection has revealed a Tablet called 'Tablet of the Spiritual World.' All who read it are filled with an anxious desire to leave this world and enter the next condition, so wonderful are the glories of the Spiritual Kingdom. In Persia, one man who read this Tablet killed himself. he could not wait for the happiness it promised him. Another, a youth of Iṣfahán, could not stand the spiritual food contained in this Tablet, and lost his reason."

"I once lived in a cave on Mount Carmel. One day I went to the Carmelite Monastery and asked to see someone, saying I had a message to deliver. They refused to see me or hear my message. I said, 'I will put it in writing if you will read it.' They still refused, so I returned to 'Akká in great sadness, walking the whole distance of nine miles."

"Everlasting Life is the Bounty of God. It is like the Sea of Reality. The believers are the waves of that Sea, one great Sea and a thousand waves as one. Again, Everlasting Life is like the rays of the Sun and the believers are windows; the Sun which produces the Light is One and the same. Into these soul-windows the same Light enters and various things within are illuminated. The Kingdom is like a garden. The flowers differ in color and perfume, yet they receive growth, beauty, and bounty from the one God and are developed by the same Divine Breeze. Truth is like the Light which is always the same. The souls of Believers are as mirrors which reflect the Light. Truth is like the light of a candle which does not vary, yet the candlestick which holds it may change. Each year the rose is the same beautiful flower although it appears in different gardens."

"What will be the food of the future?" "Fruit and

grains. The time will come when meat will no longer be eaten. Medical science is only in its infancy, yet it has shown that our natural diet is that which grows out of the ground. The people will gradually develop up to the condition of this natural food."

"There is no appointed length of life for man. Lengthen your life by living according to God's spiritual laws. Then you will live forever. This is the true longevity, the real life. The real life is eternal happiness and existence in the Knowledge of God."

"Jesus was a dyer by trade. He also lived in Egypt. 'Out of Egypt have I called My Son' (Matt. 2:15; Hos. 11:1) was spoken of Jesus. The 5th Gospel which is considered noncanonical gave other history of Jesus than is contained in the Gospels of the New Testament. There were fifty gospels, but only four were accepted as genuine by the priesthood."

"Spirit is the highest and supreme development of the soul. Soul is the material or outer self—the Mind. Mind is the action of the Soul's powers. The Body is the physical covering or medium in which Mind acts and functions. At death everything but Spirit is destroyed and becomes extinct."

"The Prophets and Holy Men always went into the wilderness to pray. Many of them walked upon Mount Carmel and communed with God."

"True Religion has nothing to do with human imagination. God's Will is independent of human opinion.

Personal ideas and mere human prejudice are the great obstacles to spiritual growth. For instance, some difference of opinion arises between two believers in God. Each expects the Lord to support his view of the question. The Word of God is perfect and arbitrary in Its perfection. When there is difference of view there is absence of the Spirit. The Word is the only Standard of Truth. Discord and disagreement are impossible among those who adhere to the Manifestation and sever themselves from human opinion. There are no 'heads' in this Cause; all are 'Servants.'"

"If all the world should combine to overthrow the Covenant, it could not succeed. 'Abdu'l-Bahá loves all no matter how they turn away from Him. Whether they love or hate Him, go or come, He never changes in His love for them. The Blessed Perfection has left nothing undone. What He ordained can never be set aside."

"Everything in life ministers to our development. Our lesson is to study and learn. Money and difficulties are alike advantages to us. Tests are either stumbling blocks or stepping-stones, just as we make them."

"The Prophets of the Word could not sin. They possess the power and will to violate the Will of God, but the desire to do so is never present in them. Knowing the perfect fruit of Oneness, they have no inclination toward that which is imperfect. Like beautiful flowers, they do not change in beauty even when surrounded by foul conditions."

"There are two kinds of suffering, one subtle, the other gross. The subtle suffering is hatred, anger, fear, and torment which follow evil actions of the soul. The gross suffering is imprisonment, chastisement, and physical pain of martyrdom."

"At the time of Muḥammad, He sanctioned war for the preservation of the lives of His followers. The laws of individual justice were confused and preliminary in the souls of men. Therefore, the law of general justice of the community was revealed by this Prophet. He commanded His followers to carry the Religion of God by the sword. When a man is about to take poison, it is right to dash the cup from his hand even with extreme violence. It will inflict injury but at the same time save his life. There must be a law to prevent the wolves from destroying the lambs at such a period of religious history. That is why the Shepherd sanctioned such vigorous protection for the sheep. Behind such laws of a Manifestation there is always a supreme wisdom."

During dinner 'Abdu'l-Bahá ate entirely with His fingers. After awhile He said, "In the East there are many peoples who never use a knife or fork. To eat with their fingers is custom among them, just as the Western nations have their own peculiar customs. We must each view with respect the customs of the other. There is a kind of food which needs neither knife nor fork and of which every one may partake with perfect ease and benefit. It is the food spiritual. This food brings life and stimulation instead of indolence and apathy. It brings peace and content to the one who

11

partakes of it; the more food, the more joy and peace. For the Spirit is always eager to furnish sustenance to the soul."

—————

"Allusion cannot convey what Reality teaches. Christ said, 'What has happened in the past will happen again in the future.' The reason of this is that all things are under the operation of Divine Law which is the same today, yesterday, and forever. By this the spiritual eye may discern that which is authentic in the Scriptures."

—————

"Sow the seeds of love in the heart and not the seeds of hatred. The reflection in the glass proves whether we are laughing or frowning. By our actions we reveal what is growing in the heart. Actions are mirrors of the soul."

—————

"These are precious and wonderful days in 'Akká. Each day is as a year. Your visit cannot be measured merely by the length of time you have been here. The real spiritual visit will be after you have gone. Some who remain but one day go away filled and enkindled with the Spirit of God. They are like the dry wood which bursts into flame as soon as it touches the fire. So it is with a lamp; the oil within it responds instantly to the fire and gives forth light. The soul which possesses sight can see in a moment, while the blind never see. An awakened soul is like a precious pearl in the midst of a load of pebbles which have but little value. To some it is given to hear and know the Message of Life in a short time, while others hear and receive nothing even though they make a long stay in this holy place."

"We should not be occupied with our failings and weakness, but concern ourselves about the Will of God so that It may flow through us, thereby healing these human infirmities."

"Faith is not so much what we believe as what we carry out."

"In America you have only received a taste of the spiritual food which is to come to you. Some will arise to serve the Cause of God in your land who will sacrifice themselves entirely. They will be given great power from God when they come forth to do His Will. Concentrate the soul upon God so that it may become as a fountain pouring out the Water of Life to a thirsty world. Live up to the principles of Sacrifice. The world will then become as nothing and be without power to attract you away from God. Sacrifice your will to the Will of God. The Kingdom is attained by the one who forgets self. Everything becomes yours by Renunciation of everything. A lion, wolf, and fox went hunting. They captured a wild ass, a gazelle, and a hare. The lion said to the wolf, 'Divide the spoil.' The wolf said, 'That is easy; the ass for yourself, the gazelle for me, and the hare for the fox.' The lion bit off the wolf's head saying, 'You are not a good divider.' Then turning to the fox, he said, 'You divide!' The fox said, 'The ass, the gazelle, and the hare are yours!' The lion looking at him, said, 'Because you have accounted yourself as nothing, you may take all the prey.'"

"The miracles of Christ were spiritual teachings, not literal."

"What is true greatness in man?"
"His spiritual attributes. No one can destroy his spiritual qualities; they are from God."

"Tests are like fire which purifies."

"How will the masses be benefited by this Revelation?"
"The Revelation of Bahá'u'lláh contains all the great laws and principles of social government. The basis of God's perfect laws is love for humanity and help for human needs. If all people followed this Revelation, the masses would be immeasurably uplifted and the Cause of God glorified. This development of humanity will be gradual, not sudden. It will surely come to pass; it is impossible to swim against the current of Niagara. Teaching the Truth is like building bridges by which humanity may cross over the current which threatens. The world must come to know the Word in Christ. How He was mocked, scorned, and laughed at, yet His mission was to uplift the very world which refused Him. Realization of this will bring tears to the eyes of those who deny Him, cause them to grow silent and thoughtful. Christ is always Christ."

"What is the best way to benefit humanity?"
"Guidance to God. What is dearer to man than life?

14

So, therefore, leading a soul to Eternal Life is the greatest blessing and benefit you can bestow upon that soul."

"When does our responsibility cease in giving the Message?"

"When we give the Message, we develop ourselves. Our own heart is opened when we teach the heart of the listener. The more we give, the more we get. Therefore, as this is the means of our own development we should never cease teaching. Our responsibility remains as long as we have a listener."

"What is the best thing to do when met by a difficult question?"

"A sincere worker in the Cause of God is always assisted by the Divine Spirit when such questions arise. The Truth will flow through you if you stand in the right attitude toward the Truth. In the Spiritual Station you will never be without the Knowledge necessary to answer a question. With Spiritual food the capacity to know increases with the will to serve."

"What is sacrifice?"

"Giving up everything in the Cause of God and following His Will no matter where it leads. We must not have desire for anything else but God. We must entirely forget self. To be perfected we must give up everything in the cause of God, judgment, reason, will, everything. To hold back anything is to be imperfect. The thing we hold most dear is the thing to give. This is real sacrifice."

"Upon which finger should the ring with the Greatest Name be worn?"

"The right hand is the hand of honor. In the East, wearing it upon this hand attracts attention and causes comment. But the real place to wear the Greatest Name is in the heart."

"What is prayer, attitude or word?"

"Prayer is both attitude and word; it depends upon the soul-condition. It is like a song; both words and music make the song. Sometimes the melody will move us, sometimes the words."

"What will be the future of this Teaching?"

"Know and realize the greatness of the Cause into which you have entered. Look not at the present. The day will come when there will not be a house which does not contain a believer in this Revelation. One Book or Tablet of the Blessed Perfection is more comprehensive than fifty volumes of the world's greatest wisdom. The Books and Words of God have been sealed and the meanings locked. All the sacred mysteries were sealed, but now Bahá'u'lláh has broken the seals, revealed the meanings, and we can understand the Realities."

"My greatest wish is to teach this Message."

'Abdu'l-Bahá said, "I will pray God to assist you. It has often happened that one who is not able to teach would be sent forth, and when the time came, that one would be found powerful and eloquent. One man of this kind in the East has even written a book. Two Jewish children have written a beautiful commentary

16

proving the Cause of Christ, Muḥammad, and the Blessed Perfection. Two unbelievers in the Center of the Covenent have recently returned and are serving with zeal in the Vineyard of God."

"Belief in this Revelation is a priceless spiritual blessing. Just as a child will give up a jewel of great price for a sugarplum, so men will exchange the Truth for a treasure of earth. The Báb said, 'One glance from the Eye of Him Whom God shall Manifest is worth all the wealth of the world.' In this one look we can attain life everlasting, resurrection from the dead, and the treasures of Heaven."

"The Revelation of Bahá'u'lláh is not mere history; it is the Voice and Will of God. If we guard the seed of Immortality, it will bring forth the tree of Eternal Life. This is the true realization of the Manifestation's Coming. His Mission is accomplished when we enter the Spiritual Kingdom and attain Immortality. God be praised! This is the Spiritual Sight. Peter perceived Christ when thousands of Jews saw Him not. Peter reached that Station at once. This Knowledge is the glance from the Eye of God. It is more precious than all the wealth of the world."

————

'Abdu'l-Bahá visited us in the afternoon. He said, "Speech is necessary and good between soul and soul. Nothing of this world is eternal. The highest longing and ambition of some people is to be a king or queen; but at the last even the great ones of earth must perish. Even the earthly personality of Jesus has come and gone. Only by serving God do we attain everlasting Life. All our fame and glory should be in service to Him. This will never perish. Live in the Cause of God;

this is the Harmony of the Universe. Shine in the Horizon of His Will. Life is wasted if not spiritual. Be of the Spirit, not of the body. The Light of the body is the eye. The eye of conscience stands between the power of knowledge and the spiritual world. Does your soul feel as sure of God as your eye is sure of Nature? 'Blessed are the pure in heart; they shall see God.' Once I was in prison under the ground and in chains, yet I was happy because I was not deprived of spiritual sight. I tell you this so that when you hear of my troubles and difficulties in the future, you may know that I am spiritually happy. I am showing you the way of true happiness. By comparing the future with the past you may understand, no matter what the future brings forth. Firmness is the beginning of spiritual happiness. Christ appeared in Palestine and was held in contempt because He was from Nazareth. Only twelve believed in Him; one deserted Him. There were other believers, but they were not strong. They were troubled with doubts and afterward fell away. Mary Magdalene held steadfastly to Christ and made others firm. God will assist all who are firm in His Cause. Firmness is the beginning of spiritual happiness."

"Spirituality is the possession of a good, pure heart. When the heart is pure, the Spirit enters, and our growth is natural and assured. Everyone is better informed of the condition of his own soul than the souls of others. Our responsibility to God increases with our years."

The "Government is upon the shoulder" of 'Abdu'l-Bahá. He bears a burden of human griefs and troubles, yet helps all and is happy; for He has cut Himself from the world.

LOVE

"How can we love another whose personality is unpleasant?"

"See how the enemies of Christ persecuted and crucified Him, yet He loved them all. Man is like a tree. The tree lives to produce fruit. The fruit of man is love. It is easy for us to love a friend or even an animal, but how difficult to love one who is without attraction. Yet if the Love of God is shining in our hearts, we, like Christ, may see that Love reflected in every personality, and love all alike."

"What is the difference between universal and individual love?"

"We must love all humanity as the children of God. Even if they kill us, we must die with love for them. It is not possible for us to love everybody with a personal love, but we must love all humanity alike. Man is capable of attaining a supreme station. Through the manifestation of Love God created Man. To attain a supreme station man must reflect the Love of God."

"There are many stages or kinds of Love. In the beginning God, through His Love, created man. Man is the highest product of His Love, and the purpose of man's existence is to reflect this Love of God in his soul. But man in his egotism and love of self turns away from his Creator and thereby prevents the accomplishment of the Divine Plan. The Manifestations appear to show man the way to God through Love. By them, man is brought to the condition of

20

severance from his egotism and being absorbed into the Ocean of Love Divine. The three stages of Love are therefore:

    1st—God's Love for man.
    2nd—Man's love for self.
    3rd—Man's love for God."

"There is a profound, a Divine Wisdom in Love. The Light of God shines in the eyes when the heart is pure. The home of Religion is the heart."

SOUL AND SPIRIT

(Compiled from 'Abdu'l-Bahá's Teachings)

Soul is the human will to live temporally.
Spirit is the Divine Will to live forever.
Salvation is the quickening of soul into Spirit.
All souls are alike in essence or quality as created.
Owing to environment, soul-needs differ; rich and
poor, wise and ignorant, etc. Environment has its dark
side and its light side. Development has its good
aspects and bad aspects. Sin is the absence of Righteousness. Righteousness is doing the Will of God. All
souls have a free will to choose or refuse the Will of
God. Each soul has its station of individuality in
which it may develop itself, but a soul cannot leave its
own station for another station or individuality. Man
accomplishes his true growth when the soul develops
in its own station. His station does not change; simply his capacity for knowing God is increased and
developed. Knowledge of God is the only spiritual
development. The Power of the Manifestations of God
is beyond question inasmuch as human development
invariably follows their Teachings. This development
is unmistakably toward a higher existence. Every
Manifestation teaches the Existence of God. As their
Power is evident their Knowledge must likewise be
true. The soul can prove the Existence of God through
its intellectual powers, but the true perception of God
is through the spiritual eye of the soul. This Knowl-

22

edge transcends mere mental proof; it is spiritual Sight; it is Vision. The atheist has intelligence of the mere mind. His words denying the existence of God are in reality evidence that God exists. The atheist's real station of development is not ours to judge or estimate. Spirit is Oneness of vision and Knowledge. The mind has many attributes or powers. The Spirit is Conscious Perception. When all the powers of the soul work together and are concentrated upon God, the soul has its highest employment. Spirit is like the Sun, the Source of all Light, alone in Its Station. The mind or soul has many lights, as the stars. The mind or soul manifests itself throughout the whole body in perfect harmony. The Spirit or Spirit of God manifests Itself throughout the whole body of the universe and is in perfect harmony wherever manifest. A wicked soul is the only thing out of harmony in the universe. As it does not come into the flow of the Divine Will, it is not of the Spirit. This failure of the soul has led man to believe that God will give the wicked soul another opportunity by allowing it to return in another body and atone for its failure. There is no proof of this outside or inside the Holy Book of Scriptures. Whatever is the destiny of the wicked soul in the hereafter, we know that its development rests with the Mercy of God. A wicked soul, lacking development, is nonexistent spiritually, just as in the station of the tree, the stone is nonexistent because the stone lacks the powers and development of the tree. Therefore, a soul which continues in a condition of nondevelopment through violating the Will of God suffers extinction and is spiritually nonexistent. The fields and flowers of the Spiritual Realm are pointed out to us by the Manifestations who walk amid their glories. It remains for the soul of man to follow them in these paths of eternal life, through the exercise of its own human will.

THE HOUSE OF JUSTICE

"The House of Justice must be obeyed in all things because it has been established by the Blessed Perfection. The Council of Constantine decided many things wisely, but its power and influence did not continue because it was not established by Christ Himself. It was founded upon the Words of Christ interpreted according to the ideas of men. The House of Justice will be appointed by the people. It must be obeyed because it is the Law of God expressed through the people by their own will and voice."

"In this Day we are near to the Source of true Religion and the Law of God, before Revelation has been corrupted by the interpretations of men. The true believer is the one who follows the Manifestation of God in all things. After the Departure of Bahá'u'lláh we are commanded to obey the House of Justice. I myself will obey the House of Justice because it is founded upon the Commands of the Blessed Perfection. The Council of Constantine did not survive because it was not founded by Christ; but in this Day the House of Justice has been established by the Manifestation of God. It is the center of true government and must be obeyed in all things. It is the Law of God embodied in the people, reflecting His Will and their need and desire, not blindly following command."

"In war both parties are wrong. Neither Japan nor Russia is fulfilling the Law and Will of God.[1] The kings and rulers of the world will find their true authority under the rulings of the House of Justice. The Law of God will be vested in nineteen men who will compose the House of Justice and render decisions. War is never necessary. It is always an expense and a calamity, never a great help. God utilizes even the wars of nations to carry out His ultimate purposes. The House of Justice will decide between kings and kings. All judgment will be from the standpoint of God's Laws. Then rich and poor will be alike justly treated. When men are developed spiritually, they obey God. The rule of the House of Justice will be the dominion of the Spirit of God. Human will brings conditions to a climax in the affairs of nations. The only solution and remedy is the administration of God's Laws."

HEAVEN

"What is meant by 'Heaven' in the Bible?"

"Christ said that nothing could ascend into Heaven except that which came down from Heaven. He also said, 'I came from Heaven and will return to Heaven,' and 'The Son of Man is in Heaven.' He said this while still upon the earth and notwithstanding the fact that He had been born of Mary. There is no doubt Christ came from Heaven and always was in Heaven, but when He spoke He did not mean the literal sky. What then is meant by 'Heaven'? Science proves that there is no heaven or sky, but all is limitless space and one universe. In this limitless space the heavenly spheres revolve and have their orbits. But the 'Heaven' of Christ is that invisible world which is beyond the sight and comprehension of mere man. It is the spiritual condition. Therefore, the 'Heaven' of Christ is the Will of God. The Sun of that Heaven will never set. In it the Moon and Stars are always shining. It is the limitless Kingdom of God. It is sanctified from all place. Christ is always there. There Elijah and the Holy Prophets live eternally. It is sanctified from all comprehension. The Jews were deprived because they could not understand this spiritual condition."

"The 'heaven' of the material world is something else. It is the sky overhead in which the clouds move. This heaven is 'up' to us and 'down' to those upon the other side of the earth, while vice versa their material heaven is 'down' to us. In the Heavenly Book it is said that the 'stars will fall from heaven.' Where will they fall? Science proves that nearly all the stars are larger than the earth. Where will they find room to fall?"

"When the heart is pure and filled with the light of the Spirit, we will know that we are in the true 'Heaven.' Christ came from Heaven, and still the Jews are sleeping. The Kingdom of Heaven is within your soul. Let all people see that you have the Light, that they may recognize something in you which they themselves do not possess."

THE MANIFESTATION

"When you give the Message of this Manifestation many say, 'This is nothing new—I prefer the home of my old religious belief which has been so serviceable and trustworthy.'"

'Abdu'l-Bahá answered:

"Bahá'u'lláh is the same Light in a new Lamp. To see, we must look at the Light and not at the Lamp. This is Spiritual Sight. The sun is one orb, but it has different rising-points on the horizon. One point was Jesus, one Moses, one Bahá'u'lláh, and so on. Therefore, be a lover of the 'Sun' and worship it, no matter at what point it may arise. If you worship the dawning-place, you will fail to see the Sun when it arises in another point of the horizon. Many stand at the old point and worship while they are losing the Light of the Sun in this Manifestation. True lovers of the Sun worship the Sun Itself and not the point of Its rising. They see and know the Light. Pray for those who stand worshiping the old rising-point of the Sun, spiritually blind to its New Appearance upon the Heavenly Horizon, spiritually deprived of Its Light and Bounty. The ministers and clergy do not accept the Message on account of their position in the Church. As stars in heaven they have become darkened. When the Báb arose and declared His Mission, many of the clergy who had occupied positions found it necessary to give them up and follow His Teaching."

"Many people, likewise, who hear the Message are

deprived of its Glory because they receive it from one whom they deem less competent to know than themselves. The Word of God is revealed according to the degree of Spiritual Sight, no matter who the messenger may be. Again, people do not receive the Manifestation of God because they are veiled by their imaginations. Imagination is one of our greatest powers and a most difficult one to rule. Imagination is the father of superstition. For example, two men are dear friends. They love each other so much they never wish to be parted. Yet when one of them dies, the other through fear dreads to be alone with the one he cared so much for in life. His imagination controls him and fills him with fear and horror. We are led astray by imagination, even in violation of will and reason. It is our test power. We are tested by our ability to control and subdue it. A man imagines he is wealthy. Some day real wealth comes to him, but it is never what he imagined it would be. Imagination is our greatest misleader. We hold to it until it becomes fixed in memory. Then we hold to it the stronger, believing it to be fact. It is a great power of the soul but without value unless rightly controlled and guided. Through imagination men receive a distorted view of a former Manifestation and are prevented from recognizing and accepting the Truth and Reality of the present one. They are veiled from the Light and Glory of God by imagination. These veils prevent the true Light from entering the soul. Therefore, men follow the false light of their imaginations and cling to error instead of truth. Thus the Egyptians were veiled from the Light of God in Moses. The Jews were veiled from the Glory of Jesus simply because they did not know Moses rightly and so were blinded to the one He promised would come after Him. Today Jews, Muḥammadans, and Christians, not seeing the former Manifestation with true vision, are veiled from the Glory of God in Bahá'u'lláh. One of the greatest veils is literal interpretation of the prophecies. Again, many refuse the Manifestation in His Day because they do not want to walk the hard road of devotion and servitude, but prefer the easy road of hereditary belief. Misconception of the Word of God and its meanings is another great veil which imagination throws over the soul and by which the Light is lost. Also, people inherit their belief from parents and ancestors and follow it blindly, too negligent to know and see for themselves. Negligence and apathy are heavy 'veils of Glory.' Read Mírzá Abu'l-Faḍl's book of *Baháí Proofs*, and you will find irresistible evidence of this Manifestation.[2] Will is the center or focus of human understanding. We must *will* to know God, just as we must *will* in order to possess the life He has given us. The human will must be subdued and trained into the Will of God. It is a great power to have a strong will, but a greater power to give that will to God. The will is what we do, the understanding is what we know. Will and understanding must be one in the Cause of God. Intention brings attainment."

"Do the Manifestations differ in degree?"

"These Supreme Holy Souls are Godlike in their attributes. The garments in which they appear are different, but the attributes are the same. In their real intrinsic power they show forth the Perfection of God. The Reality of God in them never varies; only the garment in which the Primal Reality is clothed is dif-

ferent according to the time and place of their
Appearance and Declaration to the world. One Day
it is the garment of Abraham, then Moses, then Jesus,
then Bahá'u'lláh. Knowledge of this Oneness is true
Enlightenment. Some see the garment only and worship the Personality; some see the Reality and worship
in 'Spirit and in Truth.' Some of the Hebrews admired
the embroidered beauty of the garment of Abraham
but were blind to the Real Light which shone upon the
darkness of the world through Him. Moses was denied; Jesus was denied, crucified; all have been denied
and persecuted for this reason. Men see the garment
and are blind to the Reality, worship the Personality
and do not know the Truth, the Light Itself. Some
worship the Tree of Life but do not eat of the blessed
Fruit of the Tree. Therefore, differences and disagree-
ments arise in religious belief. If all would eat of the
Fruit Itself, they could never disagree. For instance,
four men were traveling along a road. They possessed a
franc between them. One was a Turk, the others Persian, Arab, and Greek. They became hungry and
wished to buy some grapes, but as they did not understand each other's language none of them could express his wish to the others. So they began to quarrel
and abuse each other. Finally a man came along who
knew all four languages. He asked what the trouble
was. Then he said, 'Give me the money. I will buy
each one what he wishes.' So he bought grapes, and
they were all satisfied. They had disagreed upon a
word or term only; all meant the same thing. Terms
are of no importance. The Fruits of the Tree should be
our desire. These are the Spiritual 'grapes.' Find the
Light Itself, and there will be no difference of opinion

or belief as to the Personality or Degree of the Manifestations of God."

"The greatest proof of a Manifestation is the Manifestation Himself. We do not have to prove the existence of the sun. The sun is independent of proof. He who has sight can see the sun and prove it for himself. It is not necessary to seek for other proof. For instance, it is a fixed fact that nothing could grow upon the earth without the light of the sun. It is easily proved that without the sun's heat and light no animal life could exist. The sun's light is indispensable, its heat essential. This is the sun's greatest proof. God with all His qualities is independent of all His creatures. Look at the Christ. He was a youth of Israel, not a great and honored man, but born from a poor family. He was so poor that He was born in a manger, yet He changed the conditions of the whole world. What proof could be greater than this that He was from God? It is so strong and evident that no one can deny it. Without this Light the world could not grow spiritually. The Blessed Perfection came from Persia, which is not a prominent nation. The great Prophets did not enter school to be taught of men, yet so many things did they manifest that at last we must admit that the world is not able to destroy the wisdom of the Prophets or grow without them. Everything of God is proof against the people and evidence for God. Peter was the greatest of all the disciples. He was the 'head' appointed by the Christ, yet he denied the Christ three times. See what happened afterward! See what a power of penetration the Word of God possessed! How the Truth in Christ grew and spread all over the world! There must be a Standard. The Kings of the earth cannot stand against the power of the Word. The Light of God will shine, must shine. The great flag of Nero was lowered, and Christ's standard raised in its stead. All the kings of earth, all the learned men have become subject to the Word and are its worshipers. The Blessed Perfection during His own lifetime had one thousand followers who believed in Him. Only one proved ungrateful, yet he did not deny Bahá'u'lláh. Many of these followers were martyred with His Name upon their lips. The renown of Jesus' Name did not reach outside His own country. We hear nothing of Him from the Phoenicians. But the Name of Bahá'u'lláh reached the whole world while He lived. Jesus did not write to any of the rulers of the world. Bahá'u'lláh sent Tablets to all the Kings and rulers of the earth. When Napoleon III was in the zenith of his power, the Blessed Perfection wrote to him. If we should gather together all that the Christ said, it would be very little in amount. But consider the number of Tablets and Books left by the Blessed Perfection! Although the Christ was not a great and honored man, although He was of such poor and humble condition that He was born in a manger, yet He changed the whole world by His Power and Divinity. What proof could be greater than this? How can anyone deny His proof! In the same way, the Blessed Perfection came from Persia, which is not an important nation of the world. He did not go to school, and yet so much Knowledge was manifest in Him that we must confess that is is impossible to deny His Wisdom and His Divinity. So universal were the Bounties of the Blessed Perfection that the very stones and trees mourned His Departure. Everything sent from God is proof enough for the people of the world to accept and believe. The Manifestations of God are sent when most needed. There were Nineteen 'Letters of the Living' who accepted the Báb. The Blessed Perfection Himself spread the Báb's Message. Great and learned men likewise embraced His Cause. They were Mullás or clergy of the Muḥammadans. One of them is known as the King of the Martyrs on account of his death for this Cause. They were celebrated for their great knowledge and learning. The Manifestation of God is proof of Himself, just as the sun is its own greatest and sufficient proof. The sun says, 'I am proof.' In the ancient times the women of Egypt thought Joseph was an angel. No proof was necessary but his own beauty and excellence. The proof was himself. People of sight and perception see at a glance what the blind and incapable can never see."

"Another great proof of a Manifestation is His power to develop souls. Miracles are but secondary proofs. Our first and important duty is to ascertain if the real Physician has come to heal the Spiritual sickness of the world, to learn if the Commander of the hosts of righteousness has appeared, to prove the appearance of a true Manifestation of God. If in crossing the ocean everyone on board the ship should assume the authority of captain, where would be the safety of the ship and its passengers? It would be impossible to reach the destination if everybody was Captain. Then after we have found the Captain of the ship of Truth, it is our duty to obey Him, submit to His Wisdom, and be guided by Him into Eternal Life."

"Before each Manifestation a sign appears in both the material and spiritual heavens. It is the appearance of a literal star and the rise of a man as a Forerunner. The Forerunner announces the Manifestation of the Promised One. Before Moses appeared, a messenger came to the Hebrews, bidding them prepare for His Manifestation. John the Baptist came before the Christ. The Manifestations are greater or less in degree according to the Message they are able to reveal. Muḥammad was preceded by a Forerunner or Announcer. Before the Manifestation of this Day, as it is the full Reality of Revelation, there were two Heralds, Aḥmad and Káẓim. It will be a long time before the rise of another Manifestation. The Manifestations are like seas. Some seas, such as the Caspian, are alone and separated from all the others; some, like the Mediterranean, are connected with the great body of the Ocean itself. The Manifestation in Muḥammad was like the Caspian, alone and separate. The Báb and the Blessed Perfection are as the Mediterranean and the Ocean. The Manifestations are as suns in the Heaven of the Divine Will. Sometimes the sun and moon are far apart; for instance, in the middle of the month they are 180° from each other. But in the beginning and end of the lunar month they are only one degree apart. In the Qur'án Muḥammad prophesied that in this Day the Sun and Moon will meet in Heaven; that is, the spiritual Sun and Moon of this Dispensation will rise together in the form of man. We should thank God continually that we live in this Day of a Manifestation of God. This Manifestation ended with the Blessed Perfection. The Cycle of the Sun and Moon is finished. I am nothing but the Servant of God. Some in America are looking for a 'third Christ' or personage. This is only imagination. Some call me

Christ. This also is imagination. The Cycle of the Blessed Perfection will last for a long time. The next manifestation will not be so great as this One. When He appears, He will not be an independent One. Do they realize that I make no claim for Myself? I have sacrificed everything—My body, My comfort, My Station, all—to the Blessed Perfection. Bahá'u'lláh is the consummation of all degrees. He is the Revelation of all Truth and Light. Whereas the Revelation of other Prophets had to be spread by the sword, Bahá'u'lláh commanded that we 'must be killed rather than kill.' So He was the consummation of all degrees of Revelation which preceded Him."

SPIRITUAL DEVELOPMENT

'Abdu'l-Bahá sent for me. I found Him in a little room opening from the courtyard. He was sitting upon a raised chair, His beautiful face, majestic in repose and strength, turned toward the only window. He greeted me joyfully. Both the daughters were present. He said, "I want you to carry away from 'Akká the joy and peace of the spiritual life." I answered, "It would be impossible for me to be in this atmosphere of Spirit as I have been and not receive wonderful benefit." He continued, "God is like the calm and limitless sea. His Bounty is overflowing and illimitable. In our physical selves we are like the animals; yet in some ways the animals are even higher than men—they are more restful and composed—more trustful and reliant upon the Bounty of God—more in the flow of His Will. The birds of Mount Carmel are His creatures. They can fly to the highest branches of the trees and build their nests. From the treetops the bird can enjoy the beautiful view of sea and mountain by its power of sight. All this beauty exists for us as well. The Love of God, the Beauty of God is everywhere and exists for man if he will but rise to spiritual heights, open his spiritual vision, and behold it. Is the king free as the bird is free to fly upward? The king's head is often heavy with anxiety and the things of this world which hold him down. The true pleasure and happiness depend upon the spiritual perception and enjoyment.

The powers of mind are the bounties of God given to man to lead him toward spiritual happiness. The highest grace in man is to love God. Love of God, Knowledge of God is the greatest, the only real happiness, because it is Nearness to God. This is the Kingdom of God. To love God is to know Him. To know Him is to enter His Kingdom and be near Him. This is what I desire for you—that you may walk in this path."

I answered, "Now that you have shown me the way, I wish to walk in this heavenly path." He said, "You are near to God, and day by day you will progress by the knowledge of God toward spiritual joy. Then you will be a source of guidance to others. In you they will now behold another person; in fact, everybody will witness the change in your life. You must develop spiritual love in yourself and in them. Physical love is very different from spiritual love. To awaken spiritual love in others is to attain peace and joy for yourself."

I said, "I wish to teach this Message of Light and Truth, but I feel that my efforts are small and unimportant." He answered, "The mountain is large, but it has no intelligence. The diamond is small, but it is filled with light. The elephant produces no melody; the nightingale's song is like the music of Heaven. I will pray that you may become the recipient of the Bounties of God. You will be filled with power because the Spirit will speak through you. You must not bring unhappiness to others. In the future sacrifice yourself more and more in the Cause of God. Then the Love of God will grow and grow in your heart." I told Him my regret in leaving the Household where everything is in such peace and harmony. He said, "You are always here in spirit; you will never be absent now."

I asked, "What shall I say to those who state that they are satisfied with Christianity and do not need this present Manifestation?" He answered, "Let them alone. What would they do if a former king had reigned and a new king was now seated upon the throne? They must acknowledge the new king, or they are not true subjects of the Kingdom. Last year there was a springtime. Can a man say, 'I do not need a new springtime this year—the old springtime is enough for me'? No! the new spring must come to fill the earth with beauty and brightness. The sun rose this morning. Shall we say to the sun, 'Go away! We do not need you this morning; you were here yesterday'? If we strive to upbuild this Cause with faith and love in our hearts, it will overpower all the science, philosophy, and metaphysics of this Day. I Myself am surprised at the wonderful things that are happening. The Word of God shows such power and penetration that all will be surprised and astonished at Its advance."

I said, "I will pray to be assisted and strengthened." He replied, "God will help you in this." Then He continued, "Do everything in your power to help the poor and needy. Serve God in this way. The poor are the trust of God. Give the Message to every listening soul. Give them whatever they can take of it. In Persia there was a man who could not read or write, yet he was the cause of guidance to many great men in this Truth by his pure love of God. If you will turn to God, He will turn to you and assist you. He will make you eloquent. He will make you irresistible by His Wisdom. The tongue speaks from the heart, and if you are sincere, God will speak for you. Help and assist others to see this Truth as you do. Be their guide and helper. This Message is vital to young and old. In it the young must make more progress and bring forth more fruit than the old, just as young and vigorous trees yield the most fruit to the gardener. Christ said, 'Ye shall know the tree by its fruits,' meaning whether the fruits be good or bad, much or little. Those who are born of the Spirit have all the Divine qualities of growth. Without these qualities they are nothing but mere men and women; they are not spiritually alive; they are without the power of growth. Christ said they were 'dead.' Let all your thoughts be upon this so that the believers and others will know that you have the Spiritual Spring within your soul and have attained a newness of life. This is complete happiness, the only Peace. After awhile you will realize that you have been in the Presence of the Blessed Perfection. You are always in the Presence of God. Open the windows of your soul so *His* Presence may be within you."

"Souls differ in their capacity to receive and manifest the Light of the Spirit. The Blessed Perfection said, 'There are as many ways to God as the breaths of His Human creatures.' Each soul must develop according to its individual capacity. Peter differed from John, Paul from Barnabas, yet all of them were filled with the Light of the Spirit of Christ. Therefore, it follows that as each soul has its own possibility of development, it is necessary for each soul to stand alone before God. No one can stand for you in the Presence of God in the 'Last Day.' As the soul grows, its capacity increases. Capacity is the measure of development. Love is the evidence of capacity. When we love humanity as God loves us, we have reached the perfect station. Eternal Life is then ours, and this mortal world can give us nothing more. Do good each day, if only by speaking a kind word. Knowledge of God is attained through Desire and Patience. We must knock at the Door of Truth and seek God with earnestness. Ignorance is as much our natural condition as Knowledge is our condition of Development. A good conscience is the divinity within us that needs to be awakened and which shapes our eternal destiny. All souls come into this world through the Bounty of God and have equal right of Development. The soul is affected by its hereditary qualities, but no matter what its condition, it never loses the possibility of being quickened by the Fire of the Spirit of God. One brain may work quicker than another; one soul may acquire intelligence easier than another; but the power and presence of the Spirit does not depend upon mental capacity. The disciples of Christ were humble fishermen, while the learned Pharisees failed to see Him. The soul or mental intelligence awakes in the mother's womb. Spirit enters when the conscience is quickened and the soul awakes to eternal Realities. Jesus said, 'The true worship is to worship God in Spirit and in Truth; for such worshipers as these the Spirit seeketh.' Therefore, as all souls have capacity for enkindlement by the Spirit and as we may all be assisted by Its Divine Power, we must *will* to receive it."

"Some behold in a seed only a hard black substance,

while others see in it the life principle, a tree, leaves, and fruit. The true believer in Bahá'u'lláh brings forth leaves and fruit, proving that the life principle within him has been awakened and quickened. People are not sure of this being the Reality and complete Truth. It is bound to be true if we see spiritual growth in souls from the Blessed Perfection's planting. Christ spake the parable of 'the seed.' The seed contained the Truth. Some of the seed was wasted He said—and some that grew up was choked by human teachings. For instance, by associating with people who do not believe in God the growth of the Spirit is stopped. When we find believers in this condition, we should strive to get them into different surroundings and under better influences. They need a physician. The most needy are the ones to help first. The 'poor are always with us,' Christ said, meaning those who are without the Teachings of the Word. They are our charge and responsibility. During the Greek-Turkish war the condition of the Turkish soldiers was frightful. The people appointed a Commission to raise money for their relief. Many contributed for a while, but finally nobody but Myself gave to help them. The soldiers complained that they were receiving less and less assistance. The Governor replied to them that all they were getting came from the hand of 'Abbás Effendi and that all other donations had ceased. The soldiers showed no gratitude for what they were receiving but on the contrary complained bitterly against their benefactors. Just so we cry out to God, 'have mercy upon us,' when God is the only Giver of Bounty to us. War is a grievous calamity. It begins and ends in disaster.

A mother has a beautiful boy filled with every grace and promise. He develops into manhood, goes to war, and in an instant all his possibilities and usefulness are cut off."

RETURN OF THE SPIRIT

"In the Book of Íqán we can read the Word of God concerning the true Reincarnation, which is the Return of the Spiritual Qualities in the Servants of God.[3] In the Gospel it is written that they asked John the Baptist if he was Elijah and that he answered plainly, 'I am not.' Elijah appeared long before Jesus. When the Christ came, He was veiled in a cloud from the eyes of the Jews. A voice came out of the cloud saying, 'This is my Beloved Son.' Clouds and darkness gradually obscure all the former Manifestations. Although they are promised and expected, they are refused during their earthly life on account of the spiritual blindness of the people. Elijah came but was not recognized in John. It was not the person or entity of Elijah but his perfection and qualities which John embodied. The flowers of last year will come again this year. We can say they have returned—not the actual substance of the former flowers, but their color, perfume, and perfection have returned. Some are awaiting the coming of Christ in the clouds of heaven. He has already come in the heart if you believe, while those who do not believe in the Revelation of Bahá'u'lláh cannot see Him on account of clouds and veils. Many people are going out of the churches dissatisfied with religious teaching. It is because they do not see spiritually."

SPIRITUAL RELATIONSHIP

At dinner a violent rainstorm swept in from the sea.

"May we all live in the Sea of Reality and be filled with the Love of God. Thank God we are in the Ark of the Covenant. See what great blessings God has showered upon us. How many people of Persia looked upon the Blessed Perfection, yet they do not know as you know. You have reached this station, while they are deprived. There are two kinds of relationship— Physical and Spiritual. The highest and greatest is the Spiritual. The physical is of no importance. It is very good to possess both in each other."

"God be praised! At this table we are joined in Spiritual Relationship. We are all of one family because we are under the Shadow of the Blessed Perfection. Look at the earth. Of itself it is worthless, yet it can reflect the light and heat of the sun. Clouds gather, the rains descend, and the earth becomes fruitful. In the same way the Spirit of God gives life to the soul of man, and the Breeze of God awakens the soul from its sleep. Peter was only a catcher of fishes, yet his attainment was very great. Ananias, the High Priest, was much greater in the eyes of the world, yet he was deprived while Peter received the Bounty of God."

"Spiritual Relationship is the true Family-hood of God's children. The Báb had many relatives. He particularly wished that His mother should believe in this

Revelation and attain. Christ said that His mother Mary was not of His Relationship, also that those were His brothers and sisters who were in the Kingdom of God."

OBEDIENCE

"Today we will speak about Obedience! The Manifestation of God is a perfect example of real obedience. Like Him, we must sacrifice everything; every plan, every longing and ideal must be given up completely to the Will of God. We must look to God for all we desire, all we attain. The Will of God must outwork Its Purposes in us. Our human will must be laid down in sacrifice and love. 'Abdu'l-Bahá has given everything in sacrifice and obedience to the Will of God. I am only His Servant, nothing more. All our soul-powers, our outward self, our inward self must be consecrated to God in service and sacrifice. Even life must be given if necessary. If we have not reached this station of nothingness, we have not attained to real obedience to the Will of God. A pupil must submit entirely to the will of the teacher. This is true Sacrifice —true Obedience."

"Real obedience and real sacrifice are identical— absolute readiness to follow and perform whatever you are called upon to do in the Cause of God. When you really love God, you will be willing to sacrifice everything and submit yourself entirely to His Will. Consecrate yourself wholly to Him. His Will is everything, His service paramount. If they were to burn Me, kill or torture Me—no matter what affliction may descend upon Me, I shall welcome it as one welcomes pleasure. These are precious moments in 'Akká, so precious we wish they might never end. How is the Bahá'í Faith progressing in America? After you return, the believers will be in a much stronger and better condition. But this cannot be unless they see and know the Will and Desire of God. I have no wish but His Will. His Will is 'Abdu'l-Bahá. If each human creature had his own will and way, spiritual development would be impossible. The soldiers in an army are under the will and control of one commander; therefore, they are united and can press on to victory. If each soldier carried out his own inclination and desire, there would be just that many different intentions and nothing would be accomplished. One thousand soldiers under the control of a commander can overthrow and defeat any number of disorganized troops. Without a directing will all would be conquered and defeated. Be sure, therefore, that if the believers are not united in the Will of God they will not be assisted. This is especially necessary because all of them are under the Tent of the Covenant in this Revelation. There is strength only in unity. Under one Tent there is union and harmony. The Covenant of God in this Day of Manifestation is a Lifeboat, an Ark of Salvation. All true followers of the Blessed Perfection are sheltered and protected in this Ark. Whoever leaves it, trusting in his own will and strength, will drown and be destroyed. For the Blessed Perfection left no possibility for discord, disagreement, and dissension. The Covenant is like the sea, and the believers are as the fishes in the sea. If a fish leaves the water, it cannot live. There is nothing to equal, nothing so effective as the Covenant of God to bring about and continue Unity. Christ said to Peter, 'Thou art the rock upon which I will build My church.' Therefore, all the disciples followed Peter, and there was no dissension among them. The Blessed Perfection wrote a Testament or Covenant with His Own Pen so that no one who obeys it will deny or disobey God. This point is expressed very clearly in the Covenant He revealed. Therefore, there can be no possibility, no position of disobedience. He knew that Muhammad-'Alí would disobey the Covenant. By violating the Covenant he has become a fallen branch. The Covenant was also written by Muhammad-'Alí's own hand from dictation of the Blessed Perfection who knew he would disobey. What cause of union could be greater than the Covenant God has revealed through His Manifestation Bahá'u'lláh? Many of those who followed Muhammad-'Alí are coming back. After the departure of Bahá'u'lláh all the beautiful blossoms upon the Tree of Life were destroyed by Muhammad-'Alí and must now be grown again by the Love of 'Abdu'l-Bahá. The work and mission of 'Abdu'l-Bahá are very great. No one could express the grief which followed the turning away from the Covenant by Muhammad-'Alí. We should be thankful that the Blessed Perfection, foreseeing this action, ordained a Center of the Covenant through which, by allegiance and love, we may protect and preserve the Revelation of God."

At the time Muhammad-'Alí denied the Covenant and occasioned so much grief and suffering, the perfect calmness and spiritual strength of the Holy Leaf were most remarkable. The Blessed Perfection devotedly loved 'Abdu'l-Bahá, and when He appeared, His expression would change from gravity to one of great happiness and joy. Before His Ascension, the Blessed Perfection, realizing the trouble Muḥammad-'Alí would bring about, would say, "Becheveh Áqá!" ("O to be pitied Master!")[4]

WOMAN IN THE BAHÁ'Í REVELATION

"Why are women so favored in this Revelation?"

"Women in Persia were treated badly in former times by the Muḥammadans. When speaking evil of a man, they would say, 'He is just like a woman.' When they wished to lower a man's pride, they would say, 'He is a woman, not a man.' In this Day see what great firmness and strength women are showing for God. The way to spiritual attainment in this Dispensation will be made more and more easy for women, for they are more devoted and zealous in this Cause than men. How many women are higher than men in moral and spiritual development! How much more eloquent in the Cause of God! Women are held in great honor in this Day. In Persia a handsome youth of twenty, son of a believer, was despised and oppressed for announcing his belief in this Revelation. He was imprisoned. His oppressors offered to release him provided he would deny his faith. He still remained steadfast, saying, 'I will give my life willingly for my belief.' He came from a very well-known and respected family. His mother was asked to speak with him, his persecutors thinking her influence might induce him to recant and save his life. She told them her words would have no effect upon him except to increase his faith. Then she was told he would be killed. The Governor sent him word that if he would renounce his faith his life would be spared. Still he remained fixed and steadfast. His friends pleaded with him, begging him for their sakes to change. Then his mother stood up beside him and kissed him, saying, 'Do not be shaken! Do not waver! Be firm! Give your life to God! Say nothing that will deny His Cause! Glorify it by your death! If you deny or waver, you will no longer be my child!' She stood beside him as he was beheaded, pleading with him to the last that he might not deny the Truth. In this Dispensation the women will progress more rapidly and to a higher station than the men. God will assist them."

"Qurratu'l-'Ayn (literally, 'consolation of the eye') was one of the greatest and most heroic women of this Truth. She came from a learned family and deeply loved knowledge. If Faṭima, daughter of Muḥammad, had been a boy and enjoyed greater opportunities, she would have elevated her family and become a mighty pillar in the temple of Religion. While Qurratu'l-'Ayn was visiting her cousin's home, she happened to read a pamphlet explaining the Mission of the Báb. She instantly became a believer. Afterward she was taught by the Báb Himself and received her name 'Qurratu'l-'Ayn' from Him. Some say she was taught in Baghdád by the command of the Báb. She was independent and absolutely fearless. Upon her return home, her husband refused to recognize her, so she left his house. Her uncle was killed in a Mosque for his Bábí faith, and for a time she was kept prisoner in his house. After being released, she went with a number of believers to a celebration outside the city, in a grove near a deserted village. The Blessed Perfection was present. It was a meeting filled with faith, love, and rejoicing. In speaking to the meeting, she became so inspired she removed the cover from her face. Her mother and some of her relatives were present, and her action produced a great commotion among them. When the news came to the ears of the Muhammadans, their charges and persecutions against her became violent and bitter. Finally, she was taken away from her friends and put to death. She died a martyr and a heroine. In her impassioned speech she had said, 'What God has created pure shall I call impure?' removing her veil as she said it. She spent the night before her execution in prayer. Her last wish was that she might be strangled instead of decapitated. Once at a wedding all present left the bride and gathered around Qurratu'l-'Ayn; she was so eloquent and sincere. She knew the Blessed Perfection before He declared Himself to be the Manifestation of God. In herself she was a revelation to the women of the world. If this Revelation had produced only one martyr like Qurratu'l-'Ayn, this would be sufficient proof in the Cause of God."

MOUNT CARMEL AND SYRIA

"The history of Mount Carmel is holy history. A spiritual atmosphere surrounds this 'Mountain of God.' Elijah and Jesus spent part of their precious lives upon it. 'Abdu'l-Bahá loves Mount Carmel and has often visited it, sometimes staying overnight in caves which overlook the sea, in prayer and communion with God. Syria is the center of the world. The extent and variety of its resources, its wonderful fertility and natural advantages will make its future history extraordinary. Its possibilities of development are unlimited. It is the focus of interest in world history, the site of the Old and New Jerusalem. Mount Carmel will be a Mountain of Knowledge, Peace, and Protection in the future—the vineyard of God. We will not live to see this in the body but will view it spiritually. Mount Carmel will someday be covered with great universities and colleges of learning. Then the poor will enjoy the highest advantages from the establishment here of free institutions of education."

"This is the Holy Land from whence all the Prophets and Holy Men came. No country in the world has such a bright light of Religion. The Light of God has always shone upon the world from this land, and the Religion of God has had its Source and Revelation here. It is wonderful even in its physical conformation. The Phoenicians came from here. Their great civilizations spread from Syria. Abraham came to

55

this land. Here His Teaching became known. The King of Salem, Melchizedek, came from this land. All the Prophets had their missions here."

THE HEAVENLY SPRINGTIME

"Soon it will be the time of Spring. Already the signs of the flowers may be seen upon the mountains and in the valleys. When Spring comes, there is a Divine Wisdom in its appearance. God has a special object in renewing the earth with its bounty. For the dead earth is again made to blossom so that the life of plants and flowers may continue and be reproduced. The trees put forth their leaves and are able to bear all kinds of delicious fruits. All the birds and animals, everything with soul-life is rejoiced and rejuvenated in the coming of Spring. If this does not come to pass, it is not Spring; it may be autumn. But it is possible that Spring may come, and yet a tree rooted in bad ground will be deprived of its vivifying powers. Or a fruitless tree may not bear, although the warm sun and vernal shower are descending upon it. So, likewise, an evil soul may derive no benefit, produce no fruit from the Coming of a Manifestation of God. The Divine Springtime which brings forth spiritual flowers in other souls fails to beautify the soul that is evil. In general, however, just as everything is vivified, refreshed, and renewed by the bounty of the literal spring, so every soul receives some degree of illumination and growth from the Manifestation when He comes. He is the Divine Spring which comes after the long winter of death and inaction. The Wisdom of God is seen in His Coming. He adorns the soul of man with new Life, Divine Attributes, and higher Spiritual qualities. By this the soul is enlightened, illumined. That which is dark, gloomy, and forbidding becomes light, hopeful, and productive of new growth. So in the Divine Springtime the blind receive sight, the deaf are made to hear, the dumb speak, the timid become courageous, and the heedless awaken to new realizations. In short, they have become the image of that which God planned them to be and which the Heavenly Books promised shall be the true station of Man. This is the power, purpose, and virtue of the Heavenly Springtime."

FAITH

The question was asked, "What is real Faith?"

"Faith outwardly means to believe the Message a Manifestation brings to the world and accept the fulfillment in Him of that which the Prophets have announced. But, in reality, Faith embodies three degrees: —To confess with the tongue; to believe in the heart; to give evidence in our actions. These three things are essential in true Faith. The important requirement is the Love of God in the heart. For instance, we say a lamp gives light. In reality, the oil which burns produces the illumination, but the lamp and the chimney are necessary before the light can express itself. The Love of God is the light. The tongue is the chimney or the medium by which that Love finds expression. It also protects the Light. Likewise, the members of the body reflect the inner Light by their actions. So the tongue confesses in speech, and the parts of the body confess in their actions the Love of God within the soul of a true believer. Thus it was that Peter confessed Christ by his tongue and by his actions. When the tongue and actions reflect the Love of God, the real qualities of man are revealed. Christ said, 'You will know them by their fruits,' that is, by their deeds. If a believer shows forth divine qualities, we know the true Faith is in his heart. If we do not find evidence of these qualities, if he is selfish or wicked, he has not the true kind of Faith. Faith is mentioned in the Scriptures as the 'Second Birth' or 'Everlasting Life.' In this day it is the Spirit of God, the real true belief. Many claim to possess the true Faith, but it is rare and when it exists it cannot be destroyed. 'Many are called but few are chosen.' Many believe themselves to be courageous, but the battlefield of tests and trials will prove whether they have the real strength to stand firm. In Persia some believers who claimed to have Faith in Bahá'u'lláh fell away when they were tested. On the other hand, some who thought themselves weak, proved to be heroes and martyrs. I pray that you who have journeyed from America to visit the Holy Tomb may become as pure glass through which the Light of God may shine. Be firm! Be strong! We need to be strongly tested in order to prove our Faith to ourselves and to the world. Tests are always surrounding us. They are according to the greatness of the Cause, just as the size of a wave is according to the sea upon which it rises."

THE SECOND COMING

"What is the Second Coming of Christ in this Dispensation?"

'Abdu'l-Bahá answered: "In the Book of the Zend-Avesta the Zoroastrians are awaiting the Coming of two Manifestations. Also, in the Old Testament Scriptures there is the promise of Elijah and Messiah. In the Gospel of the New Testament they are expecting the Father and the Second Coming of Christ. Likewise, in the Qur'án the Muḥammadans have the promise of the Imám Mihdí and Christ. In brief, all the Holy Scriptures announce the Coming of two Manifestations, and these two Manifestations are the Báb and the Blessed Perfection. If you look into the Bible, it is Elias and Christ; in the Qur'án it is the Mihdí and Christ. These tidings are the same in all the Holy Books, only expressed in different ways—two successive Manifestations. And all the Universe is promised these two. We must not search for the outer word in Elijah and Christ but look for the Reality. The Blessed Perfection said in His Tablets that once He was Abraham, once Moses, once Jesus, once Muḥammad, and once the Báb. This is explained clearly in the 'Book of Íqán,' that is, the meanings and perfection of qualities which were once hidden are now revealed in Bahá'u'lláh. Therefore, we can consider Bahá'u'lláh to be all the Prophets, no matter by what Name He chooses to call Himself; for all their meanings, perfection, and qualities are manifest in

Him. Bahá'u'lláh is the center of all their perfections. For instance, in Moses the world received the Revelation of material laws, in Jesus spiritual laws, while in Bahá'u'lláh we have received both material and spiritual laws. The Laws of Moses would cover but few pages, and the Teachings of Jesus could be gathered into a small pamphlet. The Old Testament contains nothing but material laws; no mention is in it of spiritual laws such as we find in the New Testament. In the New Testament there are no material laws except the laws of divorce and of the Sabbath. The New Testament contains no answers to questions of science. But all knowledge has been revealed by the Blessed Perfection in books which if gathered together would make many volumes. He has revealed demonstrations in sciences, and He is the epitome of all previous Revelations."

"Now Moses said that after Him should come Joshua. The Christ said, addressing Peter, 'Thou art the Rock, and I will build My temple upon this Rock.' Jesus spoke this to Peter by word of mouth. The Blessed Perfection did not appoint His successor by statement of tongue, but in the 'Book of 'Ahd' ('Book of the Covenant'), He wrote it with His own Hand, commanding therein that all the branches and relations should look toward the Center of the Covenant.[5] Also, in the Kitáb-i-Aqdas, revealed thirty years before His Ascension, it is mentioned in two places.[6] During these thirty years these commands of the Blessed Perfection were known and clearly understood by all. Again, in a Tablet He refers specifically to this, naming one who would violate His Commands. This Tablet was dictated by the Blessed Perfection and written at His Command by the hand of Muḥammad-'Alí. Muḥammad-'Alí has made many copies of it. Therefore, we cannot deny what it says. If it was not so, Muḥammad-'Alí would be able to deny. When he violated the Covenant, he went out from the shadow of the Blessed Perfection. Bahá'u'lláh also said in this Tablet mentioned, that if for an instant this one should disobey His Commands, he would become a 'fallen branch.' He mentioned this expressly for Muḥammad-'Alí, knowing that he would disobey and deny. He left no possibility for anyone to disobey or misunderstand what He commanded. If it were not so, Muḥammad-'Alí could do many things that would injure. As it is, he has appropriated many papers and Tablets written by the Blessed Perfection. It is possible for these writings to be altered, as the meanings in Persian are greatly changed by a single dot here and there. Before His Ascension, the Blessed Perfection said to me, 'I have given You all the papers.' He put them in two satchels and sent them to Me. After His Ascension, Muḥammad-'Alí said, 'You had better give me the two satchels to take care of.' He took them away and never returned them. He thought the Center of the Covenant would be helpless without these papers. But he did not realize that My strength is the assistance of the Blessed Perfection. If all the world combined against Me, I would still possess this power, and all the world could not take it away from Me. I can fight with this weapon forever and will always be victorious. It is a sword which can never be dulled, a magazine that is always filled."

VISIT TO THE TOMB

In the afternoon we drove to the Tomb of the
Blessed Perfection, passing out through the narrow
gateway of the city and following the road toward
the Riḍván for a short distance. Then a sharp turn to
the left toward the Lebanons took us more inland and
away from the sea. It seemed to a be a holiday or festi-
val occasion; a great number of people were seen along
the roads and highways. Bright colors prevailed in the
peasant costumes, natives coming and going in pic-
turesque little groups of twos and threes. Some of the
Arab girls were dressed like the boys, hardly to be dis-
tinguished one from the other. They wore wide pan-
taloons of a very bright colored cotton fabric, this
costume no doubt being cheaper and requiring less
material than the voluminous gowns of the older
women. We drove on through a village of mud huts
built very low and surrounded by a squalor and filth
most unpleasant to foreign eyes and nostrils. People
and animals were living or rather herding under the
same roof. Dogs looking like wolves vigilantly guarded
these hovels and savagely attacked visitors. Here and
there upon the filthy ground we saw groups of men
sitting and lying, intent upon games of cards. The
women were busily working. Women and donkeys
bear the domestic burdens of the East and shoulder the
full quota of suffering. Altogether, these Arab villag-
ers were wild, almost desperate looking creatures.
Beyond the villages we drove across a beautiful level

plain carpeted with red anemones, the Bahá'í flower. Finally, we came to the Bahjí, a very large white mansion in which Bahá'u'lláh lived and from which His Spirit passed into the Supreme Concourse. The room was pointed out to us as we stopped and looked from the outside. We entered the Tomb, which adjoins Bahjí, the "Palace of Joy." Flowers were growing abundantly all around the Sacred Shrine. In the center of the building is a court where orange trees and rare plants were growing. We removed our shoes at the entrance. The passageways surrounding this court were covered with soft and costly Persian rugs. Then we stood at the Tomb itself where the Blessed Perfection sleeps. Lamps and beautiful vases were placed about the room, loving gifts and tokens from Bahá'í believers in all parts of the world. A great slab in the floor marked the place of burial. Here we knelt and prayed in solemn silence, communing with the great and glorified Spirit which had ascended from earth to the Supreme Horizon. Then we silently withdrew to a small side room at the opposite end of the building where some ladies served tea and related experiences of other pilgrims and believers who had visited the Tomb. Upon the anniversary of the Blessed Perfection's birthday they remain all night at the Tomb, chanting and praying without intermission and standing throughout the ceremonies. During the last few years 'Abdu'l-Bahá has not been able to attend this holy celebration. After receiving flowers from the ladies in attendance we bade them loving good-bye and drove home across the flower-carpeted plain, another spiritual visit accomplished, another priceless spiritual experience fixed in our memories. Ahead of us mounted upon donkeys were a number of elder pilgrims and believers also returning from a visit to the Tomb. As they rode along, they looked like the old Jewish prophets and the Disciples of Jesus. Among them were Ḥaydar-'Alí, Mírzá Asadulláh, and eight or nine others of those faithful devoted souls who love God, serve humanity, and follow the Revelation of Bahá'u'lláh. We entered the city, still silent, still wondering, still communing with the Glorified Spirit which shed Its Light down upon us from the Supreme Concourse.

VISIT TO THE RIḌVÁN

We went to the Riḍván with the holy daughters of 'Abdu'l-Bahá. Driving through the city and passing out the gates we saw the barracks where 'Abdu'l-Bahá was once imprisoned. Then along the roadway bordered by fine trees we went until well away from the city and its distressing pictures. The roads now became rough, here and there poor-looking houses of the natives. To the right we saw the hill Tel el Fukhar upon which Napoleon I planted his batteries and laid seige to 'Akká in 1799. Unable to overcome it, he abandoned the siege, saying, "My fortune has been arrested by a grain of sand; were it not for 'Akká I would have conquered the world." Finally, we came to the Riḍván, a beautiful garden filled with palm trees and wonderful flowers. The air was redolent of perfume from them. A river, the Na'mayn, runs through the garden in two streams, just as the prophecies foretold, forming an island upon which an arbor is built. High above the arbor tower two great round mulberry trees under the shade of which the Blessed Perfection loved to sit. A fountain was playing in the midst of the garden. This heavenly spot is in the midst of a desert-like barrenness, an oasis indeed amid dry and hostile conditions of nature and humanity—a Paradise upon earth, a garden of God—for here in this beautiful consecrated spot Bahá'u'lláh spent His summers. Some day the Riḍván will be visited by pilgrims from all over the world, just as the Garden of

Gethsemane is sacred with the memories of Jesus Christ. No one sits in the Manifestation's chair under the mulberry trees. These two wonderful trees were leafless when we saw them, for it was January, and they are at their best in June. Everywhere beautiful odd trees were growing—oranges, lemons, and tangerines ripe and waiting to be picked. All kinds of flowers, violets, narcissus, heliotropes, roses, and red anemones greeted the eye. In summer golden pheasants fly about the Riḍván—ducks and waterfowl swim around in the waters which quiver and glisten in the shadows from the arbor of leaves overhead. Abu'l-Qásim, the good old gardener who served the Blessed Perfection during His lifetime, took us into the cottage where that Blessed One rested and slept. Everything there is holy and sacred to His memory, His chair in the same place He left it, and beautiful tributes of love placed about the room. We knelt at the foot of the chair while one of the daughters chanted a prayer. Then an Arab woman with tattoo marks upon her face served tea and mandarins under the single mulberry tree near the cottage. We were indeed upon holy ground.

'AKKÁ

'Akká is the home of exiles and prisoners of the Turkish Government. A few merchants and bazaars comprise its present meager commerce, although in former times it was an important market for Syrian products. It is the residence of a governor and various officials. The inhabitants generally are poor and wretched, evidences of poverty and squalor everywhere. Haifa has absorbed the business vitality of 'Akká. The city looks like a catacomb with the roof lifted up, heavy walls, a labyrinth of passages, narrow streets, and dark alleys leading in every direction. But the spiritual atmosphere which surrounds us here is unmistakable and uplifting. Here in this unholy yet holy place we have been taught that the Peace, Power, and Knowledge of God can only be attained by severance from the things of earth and freedom from the influences of transitory surroundings. 'Akká is to us a gateway of Heaven.

IN THE HOUSEHOLD

We looked again at the faces of the Blessed Perfection and the Báb in the inner room. In the Blessed Perfection is the composite of all the Power and Love of the universe. The eyes seemed to scrutinize the very depths of my soul. In that Face shines the greatness and majesty of all the Prophets and Heavenly Messengers. It is the Face of a Manifestation of God. Mercy and Love surround it like a halo. Its Beauty encircles the whole world.

The servants of the Household give their services willingly, so they may be near 'Abdu'l-Bahá. One of them is Sakínih Sultán, whose husband was a martyr. It was her husband's mother who said, "What I have given to God I will not take back," throwing the head of her decapitated child at her persecutors when they brought her the ghastly trophy. Sakínih Sultán and her daughter both serve in the Household in love and devotion. She said to me, "May the Light of God always descend upon you! May your soul be a pure mirror always reflecting God! Pray for me!" She is indeed a glorified soul, a conqueror through Love.

The ladies of the Household showed us how to cook the Persian pilau. They gave us many gifts and presents, everything haloed with words of love.

AFTERNOON BEFORE THE FEAST

'Abdu'l-Bahá came in to see us unexpectedly. He said, "I wish I might be with you always, but unfortunately other things claim My time and keep Me away from you. But My heart is filled with love and the thought of you. The important thing is the heart, and that is yours. That heart may be united with heart, Spirit with Spirit—this is the real life, the real existence. All else is earthly and will pass away. But the Love which is of the Spirit will live forever. I wish we might always be together. Tonight there will be a Meeting of the believers here. At the table they will be gathered together from all parts of the world. This is the reason of My happiness, seeing the East and the West joined in the Kingdom of God. May all the believers in the world be so joined until the whole world shall come under one rule and all nations be as one family. This will surely come to pass." Then turning to Mr. MacNutt, He asked, "What do you say to this?" He answered, "What could I say that would add to an already perfect wisdom!" 'Abdu'l-Bahá responded, "May we all be perfected in the Wisdom and Light of the Blessed Perfection." Again to Mr. MacNutt, "Will you speak?" He answered, "It is a blessed privilege to listen. I am usually called upon to speak, but I love to listen." 'Abdu'l-Bahá said, "May you always listen, always hear, always speak with the power of the Spirit."

AT THE FEAST

Tonight we met 'Abdu'l-Bahá and a large number of believers from all parts of the East at the Feast, or Supper, under the shadow of the Blessed Perfection. As we entered the large hall, 'Abdu'l-Bahá greeted us, extending both hands and bidding us, "Welcome! Welcome!" His face aglow with light. Then He helped us to our seats and gave us our napkins. As the believers came in, 'Abdu'l-Bahá clasped each one in a loving embrace and gave them their places at the table. Then He passed around the table anointing each one with attar of rose, sometimes upon the cheek, again upon the forehead, or over the heart. Some of the believers kissed His hand or touched His garment in loving appreciation. As He walked about, He spoke beautiful spiritual words: "This Meeting is through the Love of the Blessed Perfection." "In the sensibility of the heart is this realization." "God is Love!" "May spiritual fragrance refresh thy soul as this perfume refreshes the nostrils." "The Beloved of God have gathered together to partake of material and spiritual food." "You are in prison here —My partners in imprisonment—prisoners of love —God be praised!"

The food, pilau, made from Persian rice, was brought in, and 'Abdu'l'Bahá served each one, again speaking heavenly words. "This is the blessed supper of the Lord, for we have gathered under the shadow of the Blessed Perfection." "We are the lambs of the Blessed Perfection. Jesus said to Peter, 'Lovest thou Me—feed My lambs.' Christ said, 'I am the Living Bread which came down from Heaven; he who eats of this Bread shall live forever.'" "The Heavenly Books prophesy that they shall come from the East and the West to sit down in the Kingdom of God." "In the last day all the sheep shall be gathered together." As He passed around the table serving the brethren, He said to Taqí Manshádí, who has a particularly dark face, "Eat plentifully dear brother; you are pale with hunger." Throughout the supper, which was very simple in its character and appointment, 'Abdu'l-Bahá was the Servant of the believers. This was indeed a spiritual feast where Love reigned. The whole atmosphere was Love, Joy, and Peace. Sometimes when American believers are not present at this Feast, their places are left vacant in loving memory. After the rice and oranges, Mírzá Asadulláh introduced Mr. MacNutt saying, "He is one of our eloquent American brothers who has great power. God has given him the power to attract souls to the Fountain of Life. His words are like a magnet. In the midst of his work he has come to visit 'Akká. We have not been brought into this blessed brotherhood of the East and West through miracles, but through the Word of the Manifestation of God Bahá'u'lláh. Through His Word the prophecy of Christ has been fulfilled, that they should come from the East and the West to sit down at the Table of the Lord. Jesus said that the coming of the Son of Man would be as the flash of lightning from the East to the West. All the proofs are confirmed here tonight." Mr. MacNutt said, "My spiritual brothers in

73

Al-Abhá! The Persian language always seemed difficult to me until I visited the Holy Household. Now I find it very easy to understand. For the Persian alphabet contains but four letters, and the Persian language has only one word. These letters are 'm,' 'h,' 'b,' and 't,' and the word is '*Maḥabbat,*' which means 'love.' For 'Love' is the sum total of the Persian language as I hear it spoken in 'Akká. That is why I am able to understand and speak Persian so quickly. The Blessed Perfection in the Kitáb-i-Aqdas recommended that the nations of the earth should adopt one language. This was the outer language of unity. At the same time He revealed the Divine Message of Unity in the inner language of the Spirit. This inner language is understood by His children in the East and the West. When the East and West meet in the Kingdom and commune in this inner language, the putting together of mere words is an easy matter. If men love each other, all the details of unity can be quickly settled upon. Business would become a part of Religion and Commerce would be filled with the Spirit of God if Love reigned in men's hearts. Religion underlies the laws of nations. If we love each other, the Most Great Peace which Bahá'u'lláh promised will come in *our* hearts and so spread throughout the world. Love is the foundation of all unity, for God Himself is Love. Races will blend together when the will of man becomes the Will of God. The various religious systems are coming closer together. Bahá'u'lláh stands at the meeting of their ways to God. In Him the Muḥammadans are going forward to meet their promised Imám Mihdí, the Christians to meet Christ, the Jews their Messiah, and so on. When they meet Bahá'u'lláh they meet each other as at the top of a mountain. There they find unity because there they find Him. There is the widest view, the heavenly horizon. No one but a Manifestation of God can unify the religious systems of the world. No law, no war, no power of kings could do this. The Kingdom is a real visible Kingdom, a real Unity. This cannot be attained from books. It comes from the heart. In these Bahá'í faces one can see the image of the Blessed Perfection. He is here. I will take back this picture to the American believers. Their spirits are here with us at this table of Love. The atmosphere is Love. The soul of 'Abdu'l-Bahá is among us; the glorified Spirit of the Blessed Perfection looks down from the Supreme Concourse. Alláh-u-Abhá!"

Mírzá Asadulláh said that the rice pudding we had for dessert was the same kind which some Muḥammadans believe Muḥammad ate with God when He visited Heaven. Asadulláh recalled the difficulty he experienced in speaking through an interpreter when he visited America. After the speaking was over, a Bahá'í from Persia chanted a Tablet. His voice vibrated throughout the hall like the tones of a clear bell. This was indeed a spiritual feast where Love reigned and Joy predominated.

The next morning we were with 'Abdu'l-Bahá at breakfast. "Greetings!" He said, "How are you?" in English. Then He spoke of the feast, saying, "I have been taught the lesson of servitude and sacrifice in these meetings where the believers come together in spiritual joy and fragrance. My heart is touched with pity as I look upon the discord and lack of unity among men. But when the people of God, the children of the

Kingdom, meet together, we find the true peace, the real Unity, and the Love of God manifest." Mrs. MacNutt mentioned the three progressive spiritual steps—Obedience as Christ taught; Resignation as Muḥammad taught; and Renunciation as revealed by Bahá'u'lláh. 'Abdu'l-Bahá said, "I pray that you all may be assisted to attain these stations in the Cause of God." He continued, "The cause of My happiness is meeting you here and seeing your faces filled with the Light of God. I shall never forget the beautiful meeting last night. You must meet together in this way in America. Be true, loyal servants of God. Arise to serve His Cause. These are divine meetings, and the Bounties which surround the Kingdom of Heaven will descend upon you. The same Spirit of Love and Life which fills the Supreme Concourse will fill your meetings. This is a time of trouble and testing to all the believers." Then one of the daughters chanted a Tablet most beautifully. The chant was rhythmic yet without form in the melody, seeming to follow the words and adapt itself to their expression.

HEAVENLY SUSTENANCE

"God has favored us by bringing us together again at His Table. May His Mercy and Bounty make night as day and make the Day everlasting! For night and day are according to the motions of the earth, but, in relation to the sun, day and night do not exist. To the sun, day is everlasting. If we could ascend to its station in the heavens, there would be no night because there would be no horizon. The earthly things have an existence, though they must perish. All creatures have this same existence; all created things must die. The wise man sees them as perished. But that which belongs to the Divine Kingdom of Heaven is everlasting. The souls of those who are awake and mindful will take heed unto this and turn to the Everlasting Kingdom before it is too late. The outward and perishable is but the sign of the inward and imperishable. How many celebrated people have come and gone since Christ lived! How many kings and princes, famous men, and men considered wonderful for their learning have arisen and passed away! No sign of them remains, no result, therefore no existence. But those humble, meek, and unimportant men who partook of the Cup of Christ's Teachings shine forever in the Spiritual Horizon, although they were looked upon as having no knowledge. That which is of the Divine Kingdom is everlasting; that which belongs to the kingdom of the world will fade away and perish."

"The Word of God is Love. It has gathered us

together to partake of material and spiritual food." He then asked if we were "happy." Speaking to the servant of the Household He said, "Why do you bring them food? They do not partake of it." I answered, "We are so filled with Heavenly Food that other food is not necessary." Then He continued, "Many of the people are heedless of this Great Day. We are the blessed ones who Know and are acquainted with its wonderful significances. Why are they sleeping while you have been awakened? You have attained while they are deprived because they will not see. The reason of this is mentioned in the Bible—'Many are called, but few are chosen.' This is from the Bounty of God. His Mercy has descended upon us although we are not worthy."

FROM BADÍʻULLÁH

Badíʻulláh came in during the afternoon. At first he seemed somewhat self-conscious, but in a little while the Power came over him and the Light shone in his face. Then he forgot self and spoke with fervor and eloquence. His theme was "Love and Severance." He said, "Cut yourself from the perishable things of this world. There is a beautiful Persian story which tells of the love of Majnún and Laylí. It is mentioned by Baháʼuʼlláh in the Tablet of the 'Seven Valleys.'[7] Majnún was seen searching everywhere for Laylí after she had passed into the Spirit world. The lover, although he knew his search was hopeless, continued to seek his beloved even by sifting sand through his fingers, proving his devotion and worship. The story of this love teaches us that there is a deep hidden wisdom in our trials and disappointments, for they prove the quality of our love and devotion to God. Like Majnún, we must seek Him everywhere, we must seek Him continually. While seeking for his beloved one dark night, Majnún was seen and pursued by a patrol. Just as he was about being taken prisoner, Majnún climbed over a high wall and jumped down into a garden, falling at the feet of his beloved Laylí, who happened to be searching with a candle for a lost ring. When he found himself in her presence, he forgot his fears, offered a prayer of thanksgiving, and asked God to bless the patrol who had pursued him. So it is in our search for God. At first everything seems difficult.

Trials and oppositions beset us on every side. But when we find Him, in our love and confidence, we thank Him for all the difficulties and troubles we pass through. Our faith and peace have been perfected by our search for Him; our enjoyment of His Love is so much greater for the obstacles which have beset us on the way. The Prophets and Messengers of God live their lives through storms of oppression and tempests of hatred and suffering. They are despised and rejected, imprisoned, tortured, and martyred. If they did not love God and know to what a Paradise of Love this road of thorns was leading them, they could not go on to the end. The soul is like gold which must be tried in the fire and in the crucible before it is perfected and purified. In the crucible of His Love, all the base metal, all the alloy is burned away and disappears, leaving only that which is precious and proof against all tests. Outside the soul are innumerable barriers, numberless enemies, and hostile pursuers. By the Mercy of God we have been permitted to surmount these walls, escape from these pursuers, and fall at the feet of our Beloved. Having found Him and His Love, we must be like our Beloved and love one another, even blessing our enemies and those who have persecuted us. All the Light and Love you have received in 'Akká will illumine and uplift other souls in America if you love them. In our actions we reveal what the tongue cannot speak. This is like putting a candle in a dark place so that the light may reach many eyes and guide many souls. The real light of the soul shines forth to the world in our actions. The most important message for us to deliver to the world is the message of Love. Through love we form companionship, and by uniting in spiritual companionship we attain power. When this magic circle of love, unity, and power is established, our influence widens, and the number of our friends will increase. The reality of Love is to love others better than we love ourselves, to excel one another in service. To do this, all ill feeling must be taken out of the heart. We must remove ill feeling entirely from our dispositions. The Blessed Perfection said in one of His Tablets that if He knew He had been the cause of sadness to any soul during the day, He could not sleep until all that sadness had been taken away by Love. If this love and companionship do not exist, our meeting together in the Cause of God is impossible and fruitless, for without Unity there is no accomplishment. God has said, 'Because I loved thee, therefore I created thee.'[8] The elements have been attracted toward each other, coerced as it were through affinity for each other. Therefore, in their mingling we witness growth and being. The existence of the physical and mental Kingdom is through the cohesion of these atoms, and this makes the Life of the Spiritual Kingdom possible. For the Spirit, although not of these atoms, can only manifest Itself in the mental and physical, and it is by the Life of the Spirit in us that the Eternal Life of God is transmitted to humanity. Why do we Bahá'ís love one another? Because God wishes us to love the creatures of God so that His Purpose may be accomplished in them and in us. Then we are the lover, and humanity is the beloved. Majnún and Laylí could not be mated because they belonged to opposite and hostile tribes, just as Romeo and Juliet came from different families which bitterly hated each other. Finally, the love of Majnún grew so strong that he wandered away into the wilderness where a dog crossed his path. Weeping, he stopped and caressed the creature, for it had once belonged to Laylí. If the earthly love was so strong in Majnún, how much stronger should our spiritual love be for each other! In everything we must strive to find God. Our love for 'Abdu'l-Bahá must bring peace, harmony, and goodwill everywhere among ourselves. The foundation of all existence is Love, and the foundation of Love is God. What would there be in this world without love? The Blessed Perfection said, 'The reason I have suffered all these tribulations is that Love should be established among the friends of God.' They asked Majnún, 'Why do you love the earth?' 'Because it is dark like Laylí,' he replied. The lover of an earthly beloved is most unhappy and yet most interesting to us simply because he loves. In the 'Seven Valleys' the Blessed Perfection shows that some lovers of God must slowly traverse all seven stages of the road toward the Eternal Beloved, while others attain in one bound, in one step. Love is the true self of the soul, for God Himself is Love."[9]

"The sign of a true lover is that his heart must be in perfect accord with his actions, or rather that his actions must speak the secrets of his heart. Events show that Muḥammad-'Alí has followed his own will and not the Will of the Blessed Perfection. A true seeker must seek for the Reality. May the Power of God grow so strong within you that the world will become aflame with your words and all the people be enkindled with the Fire of the Love of God. What the Blessed Perfection has desired and announced will surely come to pass. When Love is established in human hearts, war will cease and swords be made into plow-shares. Then will Peace reign over all nations and kingdoms."

Question asked Badí'ulláh: "Was there communication between the Báb and Bahá'u'lláh?" He answered, "Before the Báb was martyred, He directed that a large box of books and writings be sent to Bahá'u'lláh. This was less than a year before His death. At the age of twenty-five He declared Himself to be the 'Door' or 'Gate' to 'He Whom God will make manifest.' He announced Himself to be the Mediator between this Promised One and the people of the world. It is said that for a short time They were together, but this statement is without authority. I never heard Bahá'u'lláh say that He had seen the Báb. It is not historically established that They met, but the sending of the box is a fact of history. There were many writings of the Báb in this box; treatises upon the Qur'án, etc.; also a paper entitled 'Conjugations in the Name of Abhá' in which Bahá'u'lláh is mentioned cabalistically and otherwise three hundred and sixty times. The purpose of this was to announce the 'Hidden One,' the 'Manifest One,' to the people and prepare them for His Appearance. 'Bahá' means 'Glorious Light' or 'Effulgent Splendor.' The Báb knew this was to be His Name when He appeared. He also knew and announced the year of the Manifestation of Bahá'u'lláh, who first declared Himself near Baghdád. Thereupon the Name Bahá'u'lláh descended upon Him."

FROM THE MOTHER OF THE HOUSEHOLD

She said, "I regret indeed that I cannot speak your language. You also feel your need of Persian. Persian is most important in this Day as it is the language of the Word. We will understand each other perfectly in the spiritual world. A tradition of Muḥammad says, 'Blessed is the one who sleeps one night in 'Akká.' He also said, 'They who rest in 'Akká shall be honored even though they know it not.' Again, 'Blessed is the one who has seen the One who is in 'Akká.' The eyes of the Muḥammadans in 'Akká are spiritually closed."

Then she read to us in Persian from the Tablet of "Ishráqát."[10] She continued, "The House of Justice will be established. Men will watch over this House day and night. The people will come to it for protection. They must obey its laws and be attentive to its commands. It will be the Sun of Wisdom, which will distribute Light to the politics of the whole world. The people of wealth, honor, and power must turn to Religion as the evident Light and firm fortress of humanity. Our duty is to be kind to everybody and avoid wrongdoing. The Light of the world is Religion; without it we live in darkness. The Blessed Perfection commanded all the people of the world to establish Peace. The kings of the world must unite. They are the dawning-places and rising-places of the Will of God. To assist them we must strive to obey the Laws of God. The Wisdom of God is revealed in two Lights, the 'Sun' and the 'Moon,' just as in the material world.

One, the 'Moon' is the consolation or the mercy to the world. The other, the 'Sun,' is the foundation upon which the world must build. What shall be our reward and punishment?—we ask. The victorious armies of God are made up of good deeds and actions. These are the soldiers of His Army. The Commander of the Army is Righteousness and Guidance toward God the True Helper. The King must know his subjects and reward or punish them according to their merits, so those who are dishonest servants may not receive what the good are rightly entitled to. So it is with those who come to 'Akká."

"When the Blessed Perfection was six years of age, He had a vision. He saw Himself fall into the sea. In the water His long hair became shining like the sun and spread out around Him like a golden net. All the fishes, large and small, came swimming toward Him, holding to the strands of His hair. The fishes came closer and closer, following Him as He swam through the waters, which were shining like the sun. The fishes were countless in number. When He awoke, He told His vision to His father who was an important man of Persia. His father consulted a wise man named 'Abdu'l-Karím who interpreted visions for the kings. 'Abdu'l-Karím said, 'Your son will be a great man. The water is Knowledge, and the fishes swimming about Him are the people of all nations who will come to be taught by His Wisdom. He will be forced away and separated from earthly things and will reflect the Light of the Word of God.'"

"Give the Message whenever you are called, even if it be in China. 'Abdu'l-Bahá has often prayed that His conditions might become more severe in order that

His strength to meet them might be increased. This blessing has always followed His prayer. In prayer we must seek for strength to meet conditions."

"The garment with which God will clothe you when you teach will be an armor of protection against all assault. The teachers in this Cause will be as planets in the heavens, illuminating the great world of the West. Teaching is the crown of action. This was the Crown Jesus bestowed upon His disciples. The Blessed Perfection said, 'When the Sun of My Beauty has set, be not disturbed nor troubled, for I will see you from the Highest Horizon and help those who arise in My Cause.'"

"All existence is in conformity with Divine Law. This Law is and must be universal. It is a natural order and there can be no deviation in its action. Man must conform to Divine Law. That which is at variance with the Truth and Reality of God cannot stand against the action of Divine Will or Law. The Law of God which punishes and destroys is at the same time Eternal Life to those who obey It."

"It is necessary for the soul to prove the Message and reach a station of belief through its own power of judgment. Few can see at once. When the soul is firm and steadfast in its Faith, it instantly reflects the Light. Are many firm in America? Even the greatest are sometimes weak, Peter for instance."

"The Báb was a supremely holy soul. He went to school at the age of six. His teacher confessed that he could not teach Him—saying, 'He knows more than I do.' This same teacher was one of the Báb's most devoted followers and was afterward martyred."

TALKS FROM MÍRZÁ ASADULLÁH

"Persian is the language of the Word because Bahá'u'lláh revealed Himself in it. God be praised that you have come to 'Akká! Mr. M. is a teacher. It is well that he has come to 'Abdu'l-Bahá. As a pupil he should come to learn how 'Abdu'l-Bahá teaches. This Revelation is like beautiful writing which the teacher sets forth as an example for the devoted pupils to copy. It is from God. All who teach must come to learn in order that they may give forth Truth to others. Christ's Teachings came forth after His Ascension. He was the example. By washing the feet of His disciples, He taught them the lesson of Servitude and Love. He set forth His qualities, and they followed Him. Every day of your stay in 'Akká will be as a year. This will be evident to you after you have returned to America." Here Asadulláh remained silent, not speaking for a long time. Then we asked him to talk. He said, "It is not difficult for me to talk; that is my work. Why is it so? Because I look upon the universe for my knowledge, whereas the teachings of science and philosophy are from books, and books are faulty. The whole world is my book. Therefore, it is no trouble for me to talk, for I simply speak of what I see in this great volume. It would tire my eyes to read the books of science, weary my brain to repeat and remember all they say. When I read the Book of the Universe, I read the essence of all books. All the prophets of God read this Book and were taught in this way. Those who love true knowledge know in this manner. When a Prophet appeared bringing a new Message of Truth, He was considered crazy. The Prophets are able to speak from different standpoints because their knowledge is from God and not from books. Where are the books of men? They perish and are destroyed. The Book of God is everlasting, imperishable. Messages from God are as points of beginning. They are Sources of Light and Knowledge."

"In the Persian alphabet you will find points or dots which change and form the letters. These letters form words, the words make sentences, and the sentences express thoughts. For instance, beginning with the letter 'Alif' or 'A'; then 'Alif Bay' or 'Ab'; and so on by addition of other letters and words until the meaning is conveyed. In the first point, in Alif, the meaning was hidden, waiting to be revealed. This meaning was not opened until the book and its sentences were formed with Alif as a source or first point. So it is with the seed and flower. The flower is in the seed and comes from it at maturity. Thus words gather together, make a chapter, and the chapters form a book. The Prophets from the Point of Oneness with God composed a Holy Book. The world is a book. It proceeds from the Point of Oneness. The Báb said, 'I am the point of the Book of the World.'"

"All things are good if we see aright. A flower is beautiful; we desire to smell it and possess it. When we see something ugly, we wish to get away from it. Once we possess something good, it is always beautiful. Therefore, Truth and Righteousness are forever beautiful. The Prophets came into the world as living examples so the people might acquire their good qualities and perfections. The Riḍván is not in its full beauty at this season of the year; but when its flowers are in bloom, when you breathe their many and varied fragrances which fill the air in summer, when you look upon their lovely, glorious faces—you are made happy—all your senses are delighted. Your nostrils are saluted by the heavenly odors, your eyes are greeted by matchless colors, you taste delicious fruits, you hear the sweet song of the birds. All this beauty is for your benefit, intended to make you happy. Then why not praise God for the beauty of the garden in which everything praises God! But if you go to another place which does not contain these beauties, you wish to hurry away immediately, for instance, a swamp infested with gnats and mosquitoes. This is only natural. Thus it is with the people of God who show forth the Beauty and Graces of God in their attitude toward humanity. We long to be with them. We love the beauty of their good qualities. They refresh our spiritual senses. We are filled with their beauty. They are the flowers and fruits in the Garden of Abhá, Riḍván of the Blessed Perfection."

"Now I will tell you something about an orange. It will encourage you as a teacher in this Truth. For each one you teach will be the means of leading twenty others into the same pure Light. Out of one seed, by planting, you may produce one thousand oranges, the outcome increasing in greater and greater proportion. So it is with the Word of God. A teacher drops a seed. The one he teaches teaches another, and in the end the outcome of your planting will be one thousand believers. If this increase is certain in the vegetable kingdom, how much higher and greater the result in the kingdom of men!"

"Just as the description of 'Akká by one who has lived here is different from your own impressions as you drive through these streets and actually see for yourself, so it is with the real disciples of 'Abdu'l-Bahá. Without knowing the question asked Him, I gather from what He says the attitude of the seeker. His words cover every phase of a question. A perfect discourse must meet and fill everybody's requirements. To teach aright one must wander through the wilderness of human ideas as I have done. Then you will learn the secret of teaching by meeting all sorts of people and discussing and answering every kind of question. No one loves to teach more than I do with my own tongue. But the Truth and Reality of Interpretation must be given according to the form of 'Abdu'l-Bahá's Teaching. The one desire of a teacher should be to reflect the Truth as a mirror. On the face of the listener, the teacher should see what is needed and desired so that he may give forth that which will confirm, strengthen, and develop the one taught. That is to say, there is a key of knowledge which will unlock any door and enable us to enter with the Message of Truth. This may sound difficult, but it is easy to prove if you possess it. You must lead the seeker into the right road, then progress is straight ahead. In Chicago I taught many ladies. I will now give you a beautiful lesson, for you are a comparatively new believer, a new child in the Kingdom of Al-Abhá. Human hearts are like mirrors, and their Light is the Knowledge of God. If the Light should be dim, the mirror cannot reflect the Knowledge of God. But the Light of God is never dim. We can always depend upon its standard purity and power. Depend upon the Light, and it will always increase in power and illumination to you. The great need is to keep the mirror polished and clean and its face always turned toward the Light. When the mirror is pure, you will have perfect knowledge, full power, and true Light. The more Faith one has in the heart, the more the mirror is kept turned toward God and the more fixed the soul becomes upon God. The greater the firmness, the greater the understanding. Then the greater the Peace, and so on. If you do not grow after you see the Light shining from your words, it is your own neglect and failure. The Spirit of man is the cradle of the Lord. In it there comes the new birth, the new being which is to live forever. If you teach but a few souls, you have attained to spiritual greatness. From each one you will gain a hundred spiritual children. You are in the Kingdom. Gratitude and love will guide them to you. You will be like a lamp. The souls you have illumined have been lighted from your flame. You will be the focus of the rays, the center from which they come. Christ taught Peter. Peter planted the seed, and a thousand souls arose in the Kingdom of Christ. The Blessed Perfection would teach one soul, and from that one a multitude would be raised up. When the heart is pure, it will be guided and directed in the Truth, and power to teach will be given to you."

"Sometimes in America I had no one to translate for me. To speak in the language of Love we must have an instrument through which that Love may manifest itself. Love lives in the heart, even if one tries to hide it and is unwilling to speak it forth. Love in the heart becomes evident and speaks in our actions. For instance, suppose I have a strong desire to perform some action. Can I do it without the hand to carry out my desire? It is through actions that qualities and attributes express themselves. The rose is revealed through its color, perfume, and outer beauty. Knowledge is our greatest possession, but we cannot give it to others without speech or writing. If we do not express it in this way, it remains hidden and unrevealed. Take for instance a quality like mercy or generosity. If we do not use the tongue and bring forth these attributes, they are hidden, concealed. Therefore, all the human and divine qualities become visible through the powers God has given to man and through the Powers God Himself possesses. The tongue, the eyes, the ears are necessary to perfect man and enable him to express Reality. God created man with the intention that man should perfect his powers. If we did not possess these qualities and the powers to express them, we could not reflect the Work of God. God has said through His Manifestation, 'I have created man, and through man My likeness is revealed.' Man can, therefore, attain a very high station by reflecting the attributes of God. This power of expression is the Spirit."

"Independence is man's greatest gift. The knowledge of good and evil makes us responsible. Otherwise, we would be as the angels who are messengers of Divine Purpose. So it came to pass that man was made of the dust and from the earth he should appear and be developed into a high station. This is reflected everywhere in creation. The eyes, ears, all the body of man evidence this high purpose."

"A child's knowledge does not depend upon the size of a child but upon the capacity of its mind. A mountain is very large, but it does possess understanding. A bird is small by comparison, yet it has life and the power of flight which the mountain has not. Do not look at your own inability and shortcomings when you wish to teach this Truth. Look at the Power and Bounty of God, which are limitless. When man looks at himself, the view is hopeless because he sees no ability and capacity in himself alone. But when he looks at the Bounty of God, he is encouraged, strengthened, and feels that nothing is too great for his accomplishment. The birds which fly above Mount Carmel can reach the upper regions of the atmosphere, inhale the breezes of life, and view the beauty which the creatures below cannot enjoy. These are the relative positions of the Manifestations of God and humanity. All the fields of the earth with their grains and seeds are for the sustenance of the bird, wherein he gains his food without sowing or planting. These things are provided by God. In the same way man has reasonable sustenance and pleasure, for God's Bounties of Love are in man. God wishes that man should enjoy these Bounties, but while doing so, fly into the upper regions of the Spirit. There is one Standard, One Who is perfect, One, the Manifestation of God. He is infallible; others are not. Absolute obedience to Him is necessary. The Judgment of God is in His Manifestation. The soul must be as a perfect reed so that the Breath of the Spirit may blow through it pure and free. Truth is like a lake of pure, living water. Our thirst for it should be conscious of nothing but that water. The greatness of a man depends upon his soul development, upon his drinking from the Waters of Truth. The Manifestation, the Blessed Perfection is a lake. He is Truth."

"The earth said to the sea, 'I am more excellent than you!' The sea replied, 'In what respect art thou more excellent?' The earth answered, 'Because the Blessed Perfection lived and walked upon me!' Who can understand this? None but those in whom the Eye of the Spirit is opened. In a Tablet, Bahá'u'lláh says that He understood the language of the waves, trees, birds, and all living things. How much happier are we who understand the Blessed Perfection than those who do not. He knew the Secrets of all living things, looked within their mysteries and perfections. In the Day of the Resurrection all of the prophets speak, and this is the language of the Spirit. Only those who are awakened by the Divine Trumpet can hear and understand. To those who are not awakened there is no Resurrection. When we go to sleep, we close our windows and relapse into unconsciousness. The morning brings a new day. We awaken, return to consciousness, and open our windows. Then the light and illumination enter. When a man is really asleep and his soul inactive, we may say the tenant of the house is not occupying the house and that the soul is not living there. But an active soul is awake and occupying its house. The Universe is a vast House, and He Who lives in it is God. Before the Appearance of the Blessed Perfection it was as if the Owner of the Universe was asleep. When Bahá'u'lláh came, He opened the windows of the Universal Spirit; a New Day dawned, and Light poured down upon us from Heaven. All things reflected this New Light of the

Morning. Arts, Sciences, and all human intelligence were filled with new illumination. The power of the Sun produced new Life everywhere. The earth thus awakened was vivified and filled with new energy. This is the Light which appears in the human lamp at the Time of the Coming of a Manifestation. Progress, development, and civilization must inevitably follow, just as all mankind receives benefit from a new invention or discovery. That is to say all the world is awakened when He awakes. When a man is asleep, They awake with him. Many people of the world have been awakened by the New Daylight, but they do not know from whence it came, nor can they tell you what they are in search of. They simply know that a Light has come and disturbed their slumber. So they are filled with uncertainty and unhappiness while seeking. When they meet the Light of the New Day of God, it is like a man having thoughts and hearing statements he does not understand the meaning of. You from America have been awakened by the New Day; you have heard the Call of God. You are alive and the Spirit vibrates within you. To give you a more homely illustration: When dinner is served, all in the house will gather in one room to partake of and enjoy the food. A bell is rung to summon us. The Voice of Bahá'u'lláh is a Bell in the center of the Universe, sounding the Divine Call to the Heavenly Table where the Feast is spread. Knowledge of these things is like collecting precious stones. After you have secured them, do not throw them away but preserve them in your Heavenly Crown."

"Do the Manifestations retain their individuality in the next world?"

"Man is composed of three elemental conditions—the physical, the mental or rational, and the spiritual or potential. The physical begins and ends here, the mental or rational begins here, and in our true development it has no ending. The Spiritual or potential depends upon our will to know God. When we become quickened with the Knowledge of the Will of God, we can say we have always existed and will never cease to exist because His Will is from everlasting to everlasting. These three conditions of man are from the Bounty of God and His Gift. All Life is from the Word, which is from the Manifestation of His Will. Spirit is born and unifies with Spirit by the power of the Word. Spirit is the perfected man and is eternal. The Manifestations are Spirit. Christ is in Moses. All the Manifestations have their own mental identity; but all are one in the Spiritual. Therefore, as the mental in man's true development has no ending, and as the Spiritual which is the Will of God is eternal, the Identity of the Manifestations must continue in the Supreme Horizon. They exist in their own stations forever and eternal."

"The Blessed Perfection may be likened to a Lamp which illuminates the Universe. For instance, suppose three people are in a room, each seeking an answer to a different question. Although these questions involve different points, the Light of the Blessed Perfection will illumine all of them and reveal the answers. So from Him we enjoy the fruit which ripens and grows because the rain has come down upon the earth. Therefore, we see by the Light which shines from the Mirror of the Blessed Perfection. He reflects the Light to the soul, and the soul forthwith has vision. Through Him also we grow to understand each other and to know what is in the minds around us. All souls have some oil which will produce illumination. All souls will bear fruit. We must strive to understand them and recognize what they possess. By studying the Word of God and teaching it, we will develop this power of penetrating other souls. 'Abdu'l-Bahá does not ask questions. Each one of us in His presence may have a different thought or idea upon the subject He is explaining, but before He finishes, all our ideas will be met, all our questions answered. When a soul displays evil qualities, we are depressed, disappointed, and wish to turn away immediately. On the other hand, we seek to associate with one who manifests good qualities. The Coming of the Blessed Perfection was to teach us to absorb His Knowledge and show forth His Bounty, in order that we may be joined together in Unity and Love by becoming like Him. His Word is Unity. His Perfection is Oneness. This is our goal. This is our standard of perfect attainment. The Blessed Perfection revealed a Tablet in which it is said, 'A wicked man asked, "What is Paradise?" We answered, "Paradise is where I live; Hell is where you abide amid disease and horror."' The effect of a Manifestation is to drive out all that is evil in the soul and replace the natural growth of virtues, just as Jesus went about casting out devils. An evil soul is like a stony field in which the seeds of beautiful flowers have been planted but no growth has followed. God created man perfect in powers and possibilities. Therefore, by reflecting the good qualities of God the soul will witness this heavenly growth in itself and find rest and peace in the Knowledge of His Will concerning us. A good man manifests the qualities of Heaven, a bad man those of Hell. Heaven is upon the earth because these good qualities are witnessed here and now in our lives, Heaven is not above us, overhead. The condition of perfect happiness is found when we are beside 'Abdu'l-Bahá. There you are in Heaven. When the heart is pure you cannot help being happy. A good soul is like a beautiful rose. Not only do you enjoy its beauty but inhale its fragrance and are delighted with every good quality it manifests."

"In each Word of God there are many meanings, many interpretations. These interpretations vary according to the spiritual vision of the teacher. The interpretation of 'Abdu'l-Bahá is always the greatest and most complete. Why? Because His Knowledge has descended from the Invisible Source of Knowledge, and the Holy Spirit is speaking through Him. Therefore, He has all the meanings. When a teacher wishes to explain the Word of God, he does not confine himself to one kind of demonstration but uses many according to the capacity of the listener. The interpretation of 'Abdu'l-Bahá is always the true form and the best example to follow. He often gives us a spiritual meaning and then follows with a material one showing the harmony which exists in the application of the Truth of God. For instance, we go into a factory. One goes this way, and another that way among the machinery, and when we come out we have various explanations and viewpoints to describe what we have seen. Again—for instance, in the seed, there are many potentialities hidden, and we may speak of whichever one we please. The rain and sunshine produce many beautiful colors and fragrances in the flowers. So the Teachings of God and the Love of God produce spiritual flowers of all kinds within us according to our potentialities. The eye sees the rose; the nose smells its fragrance. There are many ways of sensing the same object. Similarly, we can spiritually enjoy the beauty and fragrance of the heavenly growth in our own souls and in the souls of others. The senses act in harmony, all wishing to express to us in their own way and language the beauty of the rose. Everything has speech; everything has a language of eloquence and expression. I come into your room. You greet me by word and look. I read the same greeting in this vase of flowers upon your table. My ears listen to the greeting, my eyes witness it, my nose inhales it. The tongue explains. The real speaker is the tongue. For when I enter the room, I have something beautiful to tell you—something the ears never listened to before. Man is the real tongue of the universe, intended by the Creator to express God and set forth His Beauty and Love. The Blessed Perfection embodied all the language of existence. All the Knowledge was poured into that one Cup from which 'Abdu'l-Bahá drank. The Prophets of God had veiled this Knowledge, sealed the Wine of Inner Significances. 'Abdu'l-Bahá drained this Cup. We must drink from His Teachings. The Blessed Perfection said that the ocean spoke in its own language, saying, 'O God! O God! My Beloved!' The Blessed Perfection understood the language of the ocean. He heard heaven and earth telling the Glory of God. To know as He knew we must understand this Language of the Spirit. The Prophets, knowing it, were able to speak to all people in their own language, no matter if Jews, Muḥammadans, or Christians."

Mírzá Asadulláh came to see us again in the afternoon. We mentioned the red anemone which carpets the mountains and fields of Palestine at this season of the year. He said, "Little by little the flowers will be coming. The red anemone, called '_Shaqáyiq_' and pronounced 'Shaqa-yeq' by the Persians, is the forerunner of spring. The Lebanons east of 'Akká, where the Blessed Perfection frequently walked, are covered with these beautiful, crimson-hearted flowers."

"The more you see of 'Abdu'l-Bahá, the more you will realize the inexhaustible fountain of Knowledge within Him. He is the 'Bazaar' of God, where everything humanity needs may be found without money and without price. In Him there is always something new to learn and possess, always some new thought in His words and explanations. What you receive from Him is measured by your capacity. The possessions of God are limitless, whereas man's possessions are limited even though they be vast and many in number. So man must always fall back upon human treasures which are old and mostly worn out. Creation never repeats itself. Truth is one, yet its expressions are innumerable; and no two things are alike in the Kingdom of God. The Prophets are representations or Manifestations of Truth. Truth is fixed, unalterable, whereas everything human is changing and unstable. From death to life and from life to death, man comes, man goes, never fixed, never permanent. Human life is a point in a circle. If you whirl a burning stick around, it makes a circle of fire. Man is a point in the circle of life. He always comes back to the starting point in a process which is perpetual. Every day he is born anew; every day he dies. The past never returns. The future comes toward us inevitably. Childhood cannot continue; youth cannot be ours again. The Law of Time is inexorable. With God there is but One Reality. There is but One Primal Truth. Teachings may differ, but the meaning remains fixed, everlasting. The Prophets renew the Word of God, which has been defiled by human interpretation. God has a new splendor every day. We see evidence of this in 'Abdu'l-Bahá. No one can understand the real Essence of Truth. When we look at a rose, we can understand its form and color but cannot penetrate the Essence of Truth which lies back of its creation. Who can surround and know God? This is a proof that the Prophets cannot be known in their fullness and completeness, for they come to express God to us. How can a human mind encircle God and His Knowledge? When we look into a mirror, we see only a part or representation of the Reality Itself. The Blessed Perfection has often said in His Tablets that no matter how high the mind may soar it cannot comprehend God. That which is in a lower station cannot understand the station above it. For instance, the vegetable kingdom cannot comprehend the station of the animal; the animal cannot know man; and so on. Man progresses perpetually toward the Kingdom of Spirit, which is God and which is everlasting. Therefore, as the human mind cannot encircle a Kingdom which is everlasting, we cannot completely know the Prophets who appear from that Kingdom. They have infinite Knowledge, for like the tides of the sea there is limitless volume and force back of them.

Therefore, we recognize the Manifestations by their perfections and Divine qualities, but we cannot know them unless we rise to their Station."

"All human accomplishment is mortal; the Divine Will alone is immortal. Man is composed of a mortal body and an indestructible Spirit. Good qualities are Divine perfections reflected in man. The Prophets came to this world to show us the way to Immortality. Good qualities evidence their light; bad qualities are as darkness. When man feels the Divine Spark within him, these godly graces appear as light in his actions. God is eternal. 'Abdu'l-Bahá's Teachings aim to develop these heavenly qualities in us so that we may become eternal and immortal. The soil of the soul must be made ready for the seed and its development; then the fruit appears. As the seed increases tenfold, so both good and bad qualities bring forth a corresponding increase. The Reality of Spirit cannot be completely understood. We can simply know It through Its attributes and good qualities."

"The Prophets each had an individual mode of expression. In the outer language of their teaching we must understand their terminology in order to comprehend their utterance. Moses had His characteristic mode of expression; Jesus spoke in parables; Muhammad spoke as if God were speaking. The Prophets are like clouds; the Word of God in them is the rain which brings forth fruit from a parched and thirsty world. All the Prophets are alike in essence and meaning, and all of them are the children of the Blessed Perfection."

THREE STORIES TOLD BY 'ABDU'L-BAHÁ

"The disciples of Jesus, passing along the road and seeing a dead dog, remarked how offensive and disgusting a spectacle it was. Then Christ turning to them said, 'Yes, but see how white and beautiful are his teeth'—thus teaching that there is some good in everything."

"A master had a slave who was completely devoted to him. One day he gave the slave a melon which when cut open looked most ripe and delicious. The slave ate one piece, then another and another with great relish (the day being warm) until nearly the whole melon had disappeared. The master, picking up the last slice, tasted it, and found it exceedingly bitter and unpalatable. 'Why it is very bitter! Did you not find it so?' he asked the servant. 'Yes, my Master,' the slave replied, 'it was bitter and unpleasant, but I have tasted so much sweetness from thy hand that one bitter melon was not worth mentioning.'"

"A certain king had a subject who, having by a heroic action rescued the king from a great peril, was raised to a position of honor in the royal court. Here he continued to please the king and finally came to occupy an apartment in the palace close to the imperial chambers. The other courtiers of the king naturally became very jealous and lost no opportunity of carrying tales to the king, seeking to lower his opinion of the fortunate subject. One day they reported to the king that this man was unfaithful and dishonorable,

103

that each night after everything was quiet in the palace, it was his custom to go stealthily to a room in a remote corner of the palace carrying a bundle of stolen valuables, which he hid there. The curiosity of the king was aroused. He watched and found the report true. Thereupon, he summoned his retinue and next evening, when the subject had gone to the room as usual, the king quickly followed, knocked upon the door, and demanded entrance. When the door opened, nothing was seen in the room but a dilapidated bed, some old clothes, and the suspected servant. 'What does this mean?' demanded the king. 'Why do you come here like a thief every night, and what do you bring in the bundle you carry?' 'O King!' replied the subject, 'thou hast blessed me with every gift and kindness, far more indeed than I can ever deserve. By thee I have been raised from poverty and lowliness to greatness and honor. Knowing this and fearing I may grow negligent and fail to appreciate thy bounty and love, I come here each night to pray God that I shall ever remain grateful to thee for thy goodness, bringing with me my old peasant clothes, which I put on, and then sleep in the humble bed in which I slept when thy love and mercy first lifted me up from my lowly state. Thus am I taught gratitude and appreciation of thy loving kindness."

'ABDU'L-BAHÁ'S LAST WORDS

'Abdu'l-Bahá sent for me. I went to Him in the little room where He writes. He said, "Be strong! Be firm! You are not leaving Me; it is only your body that is going away. Your spirit will always be here. I shall always see you. There is work for you to do in the West. You must teach your husband the Way to God. Then you will both grow spiritually and be one in His Kingdom. I hope you may come again to 'Akká and remain with Me a long time. You will always be here in the spirit. Think of this wherever you are, and happiness will come to you." I held His hand a long time, asking that I might receive Light and Guidance.

ALLÁH-U-ABHÁ!

NOTES

1. 'Abdu'l-Bahá is referring to the Russo-Japanese War, 1904-05.—ED.

2. Abul-Fazl, *The Baháï Proofs: Also a Short Sketch of the History and Lives of the Leaders of This Religion*, trans. Ishtael-ebn-Kalenter (New York: Baha'i Publishing Committee, 1929).—ED.

3. Bahá'u'lláh, *The Kitáb-i-Íqán: The Book of Certitude*, trans. Shoghi Effendi, 3d ed. (Wilmette, Ill.: Bahá'í Publishing Trust, 1974).—ED.

4. *Becheveh* may be *Bícháríh*, which means *poor*.

5. See Bahá'u'lláh, *Tablets of Bahá'u'lláh: Revealed after the Kitáb-i-Aqdas*, comp. Research Department of The Universal House of Justice, trans. Habib Taherzadeh and Committee at Bahá'í World Centre (Haifa: Bahá'í World Centre, 1978).—ED.

6. See Bahá'u'lláh, *A Synopsis and Codification of The Kitáb-i-Aqdas: The Most Holy Book of Bahá'u'lláh*, [comp. The Universal House of Justice], (Haifa: Bahá'í World Centre, 1973).—ED.

7. See Bahá'u'lláh, *The Seven Valleys and the Four Valleys*, trans. Ali-Kuli Khan and Marzieh Gail, 3d rev. ed. (Wilmette, Ill.: Bahá'í Publishing Trust, 1978), p. 6.—ED.

8. See Bahá'u'lláh, *The Hidden Words of Bahá'u'lláh*, trans. Shoghi Effendi (Wilmette, Ill.: Bahá'í Publishing Trust, 1939), p. 4.—ED.

9. See Bahá'u'lláh, *Seven Valleys*, pp. 40-41.—ED.

10. See Bahá'u'lláh, *Tablets of Bahá'u'lláh*, pp. 99-134.—ED.